All Change at Reading

BY THE SAME AUTHOR

A Much-maligned Town: Opinions of Reading 1126–2008
Abattoirs Road to Zinzan Street: Reading's Streets and their Names
The Reading Quiz Book
The Holy Brook or The Granator's Tale: Map and Guide
A Mark of Affection: The Soane Obelisk in Reading
Believing in Reading: Our Places of Worship
The Stranger in Reading edited by Adam Sowan

ALSO PUBLISHED BY TWO RIVERS

An Artist's Year in the Harris Garden by Jenny Halstead
Broad Street Chapel & the Origins of Dissent in Reading 2nd ed
   by Geoff Sawers
Newtown: A photographic Journey in Reading 1974 by Terry Allsop
Bikes, Balls & Biscuitmen: Our Sporting Life by Tim Crooks &
   Reading Museum
Bizarre Berkshire by Duncan Mackay
Birds, Blocks & Stamps by Robert Gillmor
Reading Poetry: An Anthology edited by Peter Robinson
Reading: A Horse-racing Town by Nigel Sutcliffe
Eat Wild by Duncan Mackay
Down by the River: the Thames and Kennet in Reading by Gillian Clark
*From the Abbey to the Office: A Short Introduction to Reading and
   its Writers* by Dennis Butts
A Ladder for Mr Oscar Wilde by Geoff Sawers
Roots and Branches: Battle & Caversham Libraries by David Cliffe
The Monmouth Rebellion and the Bloody Assizes by Geoff Sawers
A Thames Bestiary by Peter Hay and Geoff Sawers
Sumer is Icumen in by Phillipa Hardman and Barbara Morris
Charms against Jackals: 10 years of Two Rivers Press edited by
   Adam Stout and Geoff Sawers
The Ancient Boundary of Reading [map] by Geoff Sawers
   and Adam Stout

All Change at Reading

The railway and the station 1840–2013

Adam Sowan

TWO
RIVERS
PRESS

First published in the UK in 2013 by Two Rivers Press
7 Denmark Road, Reading RG1 5PA
www.tworiverspress.com

ISBN 978-1-901677-92-8

2 3 4 5 6 7 8 9

Two Rivers Press is represented in the UK by Inpress Ltd and distributed
by Central Books.

Cover design by Sally Castle
Text design by Nadja Guggi and typeset in Parisine

Printed and bound in Great Britain by Imprint Digital, Exeter.

Acknowledgements

Thanks go to Reading Local Studies Library, the Brunel Institute,
STEAM – Museum of the Great Western Railway, and Didcot Railway
Centre; and to Martin Andrews for alerting me to a particularly
important anecdote about Brunel.

CONTENTS

Main entrance, Reading station, 2013

INTRODUCTION

Between 2011 and 2013 Reading railway station has been transformed; seeing work progress on what is the fourth substantial rebuild prompted me to research the history of the station and its train services. Thanks to *The Reading Mercury* I have been able to tell the story very much from the point of view of Reading people. It is a tale of flawed genius, politics, commercial rivalry, corporate enterprise and corporate sloth, and customer service (or lack of it). There is a lot about buildings and platforms (from one in 1840 to 15 in 2013), but very little about locomotives or rolling stock: these aspects have been thoroughly covered by many others, and there is but one solitary engine number to spot.

In March 1989 I wrote a piece for the first issue of *Catalyst*, Reading's own magazine, entitled 'All Change Here'. Celebrating the opening of the new concourse, booking office and shopping arcade at the station, I enthused:

> The new ticket hall is a bit gaunt and empty as yet, but if you half-close your eyes and half-listen to the announcements echoing round its roof, you could be at some important European junction. You are, of course. The generous footbridge trembles impressively as trains thunder under, and has grand if dusty views up and down the line.

Nearly a quarter of a century later the bridge was clearly not generous enough for 19 million passengers a year; the four through platforms could not cope with an intensive timetable; and North–South trains conflicted with East–West ones on the level. The massive programme of improvements centred around the new platforms and footbridge (or 'transfer deck') will solve these problems.

I have necessarily written a chronological account, but a number of topics that may stretch over several or many years are pulled together in separate sections, as shown in the contents.

I have abbreviated the names of the Great Western, London and South Western and South Eastern Railways to GW, LSW and SE. The GW was variously known to its friends and detractors as 'God's Wonderful Railway', the 'Great Way Round' and 'Go When Ready'.

LONDON
4.0

Milestone on the Bath Road

PREHISTORY

1800   In 1800 a Dr John Anderson proposed a railway from London to Bristol, perhaps running alongside the Bath Road. The first successful steam locomotive was still four years off, so this would have had to use horses; even so, iron or wooden rails would have been more efficient than a muddy roadway.

1824   Serious proposals appeared from 1824, not all of them necessarily serving Reading. John Loudon McAdam, the great road engineer, suggested a line leaving Bristol by way of Mangotsfield, passing to the north of Bath and thence by Wootton Bassett, Wantage and Wallingford, whence it might have gone via Reading, Wargrave, Bray and the present route to Southall, or alternatively by a very difficult and expensive trajectory through Ewelme, Turville, Wooburn and Burnham, avoiding major towns and causing vastly more scenic disruption in the Chilterns than the present proposal for High Speed Two (HS2). Both routes continued not to central London but to Brentford. Clearly the aim was to compete with the Kennet and Avon Canal and the Thames for long-distance goods traffic, rather than passengers; for them McAdam proposed a new turnpike road to serve centres of population. The promoters expected a large trade in cattle and other produce from Ireland. There were alternative routes between Bath and Reading: one ran via Bradford, Devizes and Newbury, the other taking the present easier line via Chippenham and Swindon. East of Maidenhead McAdam offered three lines, one of them passing through Kingston-upon-Thames.

1832–3   Not much came of this or other schemes until 1832, when William Brunton came up with a route via Devizes, the Kennet valley, Reading, Datchet, Colnbrook and a terminus very close to Paddington. The prime movers in the formation of the Great Western in 1832–3 were Bristol merchants; the company was at first to be called the Bristol and London, and its coat of arms consisted of those of the two cities

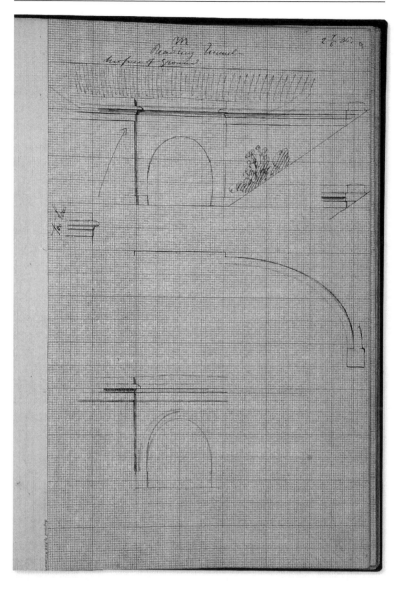

Brunel's drawing for 'Reading tunnel', 7 June 1836. This would have passed under the high ground south of Sonning; a deep cutting was made instead. Reproduced by permission of the Brunel Institute, Bristol.

side by side. There appears to have been little concern for anywhere in between.

1833   In February 1833, before he had even been provisionally appointed in March, Brunel insisted that 'at whatever expense, the line must be brought to the river, either at Rotherhithe or Lambeth'. In April he sent out a surveyor called Thomas Hughes to look at a line starting from a terminus at Vauxhall Bridge and proceeding through Kingston-upon-Thames, Weybridge, Windlesham, Wokingham, Sindlesham, Maiden Erleigh, Whitley, Southcote, Calcot, Theale, Sulham, Pangbourne, Moulsford, Harwell, Wantage, and Wootton Bassett. This intriguing line would have given Reading a station (if any) at Whitley Pump, and a steep drop over the Kennet. In August the *Mercury* carried a notice of a meeting to discuss the railway proposal, and also an enthusiastic pro-railway editorial quoting from the GW's prospectus. In September the rival *Berkshire Chronicle* heard a rumour that the line would cross the Thames at Sonning and Pangbourne, thereby giving Caversham a station rather than Reading. In the same month the paper carried a letter from 'A landowner on the line' which started with a magnificent 143-word sentence:

> I have hitherto abstained from expressing my astonishment and indignation upon reading, from week to week, in the columns of a newspaper, professing to be devoted to, and certainly mainly supported by, the agricultural interest, laudatory paragraphs regarding the mischievous project which the spirit of speculation has lately promulgated under the pompous designation of the 'Great Western Railway', because I had taken for granted that no one who, in these 'enlightened days', had participated in the vaunted 'march of intellect' could be deluded into approbation of a project, admirably calculated indeed to fill the pockets of solicitors, surveyors, and contractors, but pregnant, in its success, with injury to landowners, farmers, coachmasters, innkeepers, and the manifold establishments connected with them,

and, in its failure, with loss and ruin to the unfortunate 'capitalist' who shall have become the dupe of the specious and delusive scheme.

No doubt the writer attended an anti-GW meeting at the Bear Hotel in December. In October the Thames Commissioners resolved that 'the General Committee be instructed and empowered to take all such steps as they shall deem advisable for effectually opposing the progress of both the one and the other of these useless and mischievous projects'. (The GW at that stage could only afford to apply for Acts for lines from Bristol to Bath and Reading to London.) Reading petitioned in favour of the GW Bill. In December the *Chronicle* published some anti-railway 'Lines Pathetic and dramatic, prospectively supposed to be spoken in 1840, after the establishment of the Great Western'.

1834   In 1834 an advertisement for land at Grove, near Wantage, mentioned as one of its advantages the proximity of the proposed railway; this was the first of many such notices. The buyer had to wait until 1846 for Wantage Road station to be built.

A House of Commons committee asked Brunel whether he would arrange the line so as to injure ornamental property as little as possible? 'Yes'. The Kennet and Avon Canal Company were persuaded to withdraw their objection.

1835   In 1835 stage coaches were doing 80 journeys a week from London to Reading, demonstrating a real demand for public transport. Brunel had controversially chosen to make the 'gauge' of his track – the distance between the two rails – 7 feet, whereas all other lines agreed on 4 feet 8½. But already in September he was aware of potential problems and suggested a mixed three-rail gauge as a solution.

1836   In January 1836 the *Chronicle* celebrated the flourishing state of Reading, with its new gasworks, infirmary, Philosophical Institution, police force, and Roman Catholic chapel:

> We have not mentioned the most important change of all – the new railway – because that is incidental to

the locality of the town; but Reading has supported this novelty with more spirit, in proportion to its size, that any other town on the line, and is fairly entitled to claim a share in its establishment.

The *Mercury*'s editorial on 16 May discussed the proliferation of schemes that was to become known as the 'railway mania'; it predicted that many would fail, and did not see the need for legislation, trusting market forces and investors' common sense. In July the GW invited tenders for the civil engineering works between Ruscombe, near Twyford, and the Caversham Road in Reading; a tunnel was still envisaged at Sonning. By the end of August contracts had been let for the whole line from Acton to Reading. A proposal to share tracks with the London and Birmingham from Acton to Euston was finally dropped because there would be insufficient room at the terminus.

1837   In February 1837 someone proposed a London, Exeter and Falmouth railway that would diverge from the GW at Sonning and therefore not serve central Reading. In March the GW obtained permission to vary the route to avoid a half-mile tunnel at Purley (the one at Sonning had already become a cutting). By May 1837 'Very great progress has been made in the vicinity of this town ... a handsome four-arch bridge is to be built over the Kennet'. And in August:

> [a] locomotive engine is now employed on the Great Western Railway, between the Kennet and the hill at Sonning, to convey the wagons filled with earth, from the latter place to the King's Meadow. We trust that this agent may be the means of putting to an end the rough and unfeeling treatment shewn to the poor horses engaged in the work.

Human animals were also suffering: many workmen were killed and injured, especially in the hand-dug Sonning cutting. The GW board were now confident of reaching Reading in the autumn of 1838. A year earlier they expected that a combined train and coach journey could put Reading within an unprecedented 70 minutes of London.

1838   At the start of 1838 the *Chronicle* quoted the *Railway Times*:

> The progress of the Great Western Railway is naturally watched with peculiar anxiety, on account of the many novelties in construction hazarded by its engineer, who though an able and ingenious man, has himself had no experience in railways and seems to hold in slight regard the judgment of those who have.

The *Mercury* shifted its ground on the mania question, supporting a commission to oversee a national railway plan. In this year we hear from an enthusiastic potential customer: James Morrison, self-made 'Napoleon of shopkeepers', Liberal MP and member of the Select Committee on Railways, bought Basildon Park, near Pangbourne. Soon after moving in, he wrote:

> We shall soon not want a Town House. In three years all the best Physicians will recommend a ride in a steam carriage an hour before dinner as much better than a ride in the Park, and my cards will run thus; 'Train off at 6; dinner on table 7 precisely; return steam up at ½ past 10; carriages to Paddington at ¼ past 11'; Brunel and 50 miles an hour!

Trial trains were indeed reaching that speed near West Drayton. Work progressed at Reading: bricklayers were building the bridge over Caversham Road, and someone complained that the embankment near King's Meadow obscured the view of the Thames from the Forbury. There was evidently a cash flow problem in June: unpaid navvies threatened to destroy the work. On 4 June the first section of the line opened from Paddington to Taplow. The *Chronicle* was less than excited, calling it 'an interesting, and to many persons very important, event'. By the end of the month it noted that 'It is an everyday occurrence for the tradesmen of Windsor to jump up from their breakfast, proceed to London by the railroad, transact business, and be back before one o'clock for dinner'. It also reported that the *North Star* locomotive, travelling alone from Southall to Slough to assist a 'sulky' engine, covered 12 miles in five minutes, averaging an incredible 114 mph. One traveller complained that a combined rail and coach fare from London to Reading cost 13 shillings as against 8 shillings for a coach all the way.

1839 In 1839 the Select Committee pondered whether the same company should provide the track and the rolling stock, and also discussed the possibility of nationalisation. An independent technical report commended the broad gauge coaches for their stability but raised doubts about air resistance at high speed. Somewhat academically, it recommended a national gauge somewhere between the broad and the narrow then being built. Brunel responded by suggesting that engines should have rounded fronts. (A century later, the GW did try this with just two locomotives.) On 20 July the £12,000 contract to build Reading station was let to Messrs Grissell and Peto. The only Reading-based bidder was Richard Billing, who built Albion Place and Portland Place on London Road; a design by him might have been rather more elegant than the brick boxes that were erected. The Royal Berkshire Hospital welcomed its first patient, a 15-year-old labourer injured while working on the railway.

1840 In January 1840 the *Mercury* reported that 'The station begins to present a very extended outline, but will require some considerable time for its completion.' On 21 March it looked forward to the opening on the 30th:

> We have no doubt, this long-wished for event will attract a large number of spectators, and, with propitious weather, a good band, and gay banners, the scene will be highly interesting and enlivening. The Forbury will now, possibly, become a very fashionable promenade.

In the pre-railway age, towns kept local time, which varied with longitude. Reading was nearly four minutes behind London. A correspondent complained that the church clocks disagreed by up to 15 minutes, and urged that they needed to harmonise in view of the impending opening of the railway. (The subject came up again in December 1843: 'The clocks at public institutions in this town ought to be kept to the Reading time, and not by the London or Railway.') The excitement was somewhat dampened two days be-

Henry West memorial

fore the great day by the death of William West, a native of
Wilton in Wiltshire, who was working on the station roof.
A sudden whirlwind blew him off. A memorial, which calls
him Henry West, was put up in St Laurence's churchyard; it
has been replaced several times. Several other people were
injured by flying debris, including Mr Grissell, one of the contractors building the station. The same issue of the paper
announced that there would be nine passenger trains a day
each way, and one at night to carry baggage. Another test
train had reached Reading in 45 minutes.

The *Chronicle* was cautious:

Public opinion is, as might be expected, much divided
on the question, whether the prosperity of the borough
will eventually be increased or diminished by the facility
of communication with London, which the railway will
produce; much uncertainty on this subject must necessarily prevail, but it is generally remarked that the greatest advocates for the railway are much less sanguine of
success than formerly.

Advert in the Homeland Handbook *for Reading, 1906*

THE LINE OPENS: THE FIRST STATION

1840   The *Mercury* reported the opening: 'Fire Fly started for Paddington at 6 am last Monday ...'. (A wise choice of locomotive: this was Daniel Gooch's prototype for a highly successful class of engine, far superior to the inefficient and unreliable machines that Brunel had ordered.)

> The novelty of this delightful and expeditious mode of travelling, coupled with the extreme beauty of the morning, attracted a vast number of our country friends to the town ... The station house (which is a most commodious and neatly built structure) will soon be completed, and preparations are making to erect another similar building in connexion with the shed near the Caversham Road archway.

The designer of the 'commodious' brick boxes that served as a station is not known; it was certainly not Brunel, who called them 'paltry' and is said to have wanted 'an extravaganza' of a building. No-one seems to have commented – yet – on Brunel's strange decision to have a single platform serving 'Up' (to London) and 'Down' (to Bristol) trains. In the same issue of the *Mercury* some quick-off-the-mark entrepreneur advertised 'The Reading Illustrated Letter Paper, with a new view of the town from the railway at Kennet's mouth. 3d a sheet'.

The rival *Chronicle*'s report praised the trains' punctuality, re-christened the locomotive 'Wild-fire', and seemed surprised that 'the train came in, preceded by the engine, in beautiful style'.

Later in April the same paper reported that a sightseer who wanted to set eyes on Adolphus Frederick, Duke of Cambridge, who was known to be travelling by train, was prevented by a policeman from walking on the 'terrace' – evidently the platform – from which the trains started. He had to buy a ticket to Twyford to gain access; once there, he resold the return half for sixpence.

In April the GW announced that they were to carry mails. A week later, a mail train caught fire in Sonning cutting; fire buckets being in short supply, people used their hats.

On 13 May the Quaker businessman Robert Barclay Fox recorded his journey up from the West Country in his journal:

> Got on the Railway at Reading and travelled by that mode the last 38 miles. The carriage was the most superb of any railway carriage I ever saw, a regular drawing room with large plate glass windows, and two tables surrounded by velvet sofas. The motion, however, the worst I know on any rails.

Fox was one of a very select few who were entitled to judge such matters: this was his fourth railway trip. His comments point up the advantages of Brunel's broad gauge and the luxury of first class, but also the defects of the longitudinal baulk sleepers. In the same month the well-known artist Edward Havell published a book of local scenes including 'the beautiful view of Caversham from the railway station'. At the end of the month a man was knocked down by a train near the Kennet bridge, 'despite a warning from the policeman'. This functionary was the earliest version of a signalman; they were stationed in sentry-boxes at intervals along the line and gave hand signals to the drivers. Depending on how long before the previous train had passed, they indicated 'stop', 'caution' or 'clear'. At this time trains were supposed to run half an hour apart, but breakdowns and Brunel's unreliable engines necessitated some sort of control, however crude. Later in the year a driver was fined in court for not going at the proper speed at Slough, thus endangering lives. Perhaps he was going slowly because he could not see through the smoke and autumn mist, or maybe he had a poorly-performing machine.

A further section of line opened to Steventon, beyond Didcot on the main road from Newbury to Oxford, on 1 June. The GW had two committees of directors, based in Bristol and London; for a while they all met halfway, in the grand stationmaster's house at Steventon. Seven of the 16 daily trains from Paddington to Reading continued to Steventon. By July, road coaches were competing fiercely for passen-

Caversham Road bridge, 1843

gers from Reading to Newbury; in August the latter's towns-people were demanding their own branch railway.

An advert for land in Caversham in April 1841 reassured buyers that 'at too great a distance to be anything but an amusing object, runs the Great Western Railway'. On 27 May a violent hailstorm broke almost every pane of the station's numerous skylights.

1842   In April 1842 *Snare's Post Office Directory* claimed that 'there is not a town within the three kingdoms that can boast of greater facilities of communication with all parts of the country'. The *Mercury* ran an editorial chastising the GW for their poor treatment of third class passengers. In May, a brief news item reported that 'the lady of F. Sadgrove had given birth to a son at Reading station'. In July someone complained that he was not allowed onto the platform to meet his daughters off a train; the GW quickly relented and changed the rules.

1843   In 1843 the electric telegraph reached Slough; it extended to Bristol by 1852. Messages could pass quickly between stations, but it was no substitute for proper signalling. In the same year William Henry Fox Talbot, inventor of the photographic positive/negative system, set up his establishment in Baker Street, Reading; perhaps because the air was cleaner than London's, and very likely also because trains

Mock turtle and gravy soup: the Great Western Hotel

Just across the road from the station stands the Malmaison, a plain white stuccoed post-Georgian building. As with the station, the architect is unknown. It is often claimed to be the world's first or oldest railway hotel. It is probably the oldest now in use as such, but the earliest of its kind was almost certainly the Royal Western in Bristol, designed in 1839 by R.S. Pope, perhaps in collaboration with Brunel. It was intended to be part of Brunel's seamless 'railway to America', but was oddly sited away from both station and docks, and closed as soon as 1855. It is now a facaded office block called (inevitably) Brunel House.

The origins of railway-associated catering and accommodation at Reading are somewhat complex. A notice in the *Mercury* in June 1840 baldly stated that 'refreshments are provided at the station'. By September there was a Railway Tavern 'near the Caversham Road bridge'. A year later Mr Grissell – presumably the joint building contractor – was granted a licence for 'the Railway Hotel', but that does not mean that it had actually been built. In August 1842 the Reading printer John Snare published his *Post Office Directory*; it included a view of the station as seen from the parapet of the Great Western Hotel, which by then must have been in course of erection. The following month Richard Monk was granted licences for the Railway Tap (no address given) and refreshment rooms 'adjoining the station'. In September 1843 George Bailey applied for a licence for the hotel; in October he advertised his refreshment rooms at the station, 'where every attention will be paid to Ladies and Gentlemen on the arrival and departure of each train. Mock Turtle and Gravy Soups always ready'. This facility may have been in the unfinished hotel or a separate building, perhaps taking over Monk's business. In January 1844 an advert for a school invited parents of potential pupils to meet the teachers at the hotel, which must have had some public rooms open. On 3 February Bailey announced his opening dinner on the 28th, with a ball and supper the following evening. There is no evidence that the GW ever operated either the hotel or the tavern; by 1844 the latter was also the 'Great Western'. The year 1848 brings mention of a Railway Arms in Whitley; most stations sooner or later acquired a pub or hotel, but this establishment, far from the tracks, was merely using a trendy name. Bailey was still in charge of the hotel proper in March 1851, announcing that he had 'entirely refitted his slate billiard tables'. In August of that year the head waiter from the hotel took over the Caversham Road Tavern and renamed it Radley's Junction Hotel, claiming that it was two minutes' walk from the station and enjoyed views

The Malmaison Hotel, Great Western House

of the beautiful Oxfordshire hills. In 1858 the then owner appealed against his parish rates; he had built a large establishment in the expectation that the GW would establish its engineering works nearby, rather than at Swindon. In 1859 the employees of the SE and LSW dined together at the Great Western Tap; was this part of the hotel? In 1860 William Brown designed a new wing, and in 1882 further additions were made by John Thomas Brown, William Brown (junior) and Frederick William Albury.

In February 1861 Mr W.G. Flanagan, the new proprietor of the hotel, treated a number of GW officials to a dinner. By 1865 there was a Railway Tavern in Greyfriars Road. Early in 1868 the GW invited tenders to run the newly erected refreshment rooms in part of what is now the Three Guineas pub. In November Flanagan started a lawsuit against the GW. He thought he was entitled to lease the refreshment rooms for the same duration as the hotel, and he won his case. But in November 1869 we read that 'the old refreshment rooms have closed. Rooms in the new building, elegantly furnished as first and second class refreshment rooms, opened last week'. In March 1880 the Reading Temperance Council declared that 'refreshment provision at the GW station was inadequate, especially for the poorer classes; tea, coffee and other non-intoxicants were too dear'. In 1892 there was a Railway Arms beer-house on Caversham Road; was this the demoted Radley's Hotel?

Two years later Flanagan complained that his guests were being disturbed by rowdy youths trespassing on the railway. Late in 1895 the GW announced that it proposed to acquire the management of all refreshment rooms and hotels on the system, but this evidently did not include the Reading hotel.

The 1906 *Homeland Handbook* for Reading carried an advert for the 'Private and Family Hotel, with Ladies' Coffee and Drawing Rooms, Home Comforts, Reasonable Charges, Good Accommodation for Motors, and Posting in all its Branches'. Flanagan was still there: in the 1933 edition of *Bradshaw's Guide* the Great Western calls itself 'the leading and county hotel', with restaurant, lounge, American bar and garage adjoining. The 1949 *Official Guide* to the town promised 'ample accommodation for 50 resident guests and excellent rooms for Private Dances, Dinners and Wedding Receptions'. The establishment closed in the mid-1960s after a fire and was used as offices for some years. The architectural historian H. Godwin Arnold's brief description, written in 1972, reads 'Italian, rather minor and much altered, but will soon be replaced no doubt by something horrible'. It survived, and in 2005 a plan was submitted for re-conversion to a hotel, with an L-shaped 11-storey extension dwarfing the old part. This was rejected, and in 2007 Malmaison opened, with one discreet new floor on top. The 2010 edition of the Pevsner *Buildings of England* calls it 'a quiet, small palazzo with a bracket cornice'.

would get him quickly either to the capital or his country home in Lacock, near Chippenham. He did not, unfortunately, take any pictures of trains or railways. In October a branch line to Newbury from Pangbourne was suggested.

1844   In 1844 a company was formed to promote a Tring, Reading and Basingstoke Railway, which would have passed through Rotherfield Greys, Henley and Shiplake. Nationally there were moves to set up a Railway Reform Association to press for nationalisation. In November, Parliament passed an Act obliging all railways to run at least one train a day serving all stations, at a minimum average speed of 12mph, with seats and weather protection, at a fare of no more than a penny a mile. These services became known as 'parliamentary trains'. At the same time, it was reported that ordinary, non-parliamentary English train fares were higher than in France, Belgium and Germany.

1845   In February 1845 the GW's half-yearly report announced that second class coaches were to be enclosed; faster trains would reach Oxford in an hour and a half, Bristol in three and three-quarters, and Exeter in five. These timings were soon achieved, bringing Bristol within three hours from London. A shareholder asked whether the company would be extending their line to 'the great terminus about to be formed at Hungerford Bridge' – i.e. the LSW's Waterloo. In October the mania was conspicuously visible locally. Newbury was said to be inundated with railway surveyors: 16 separate parties of them were spotted in a single day. Wokingham had the same problem: 'the present railway schemes in this neighbourhood are becoming seriously offensive and vexatious'. The *Mercury*'s four issues in November contained 151 references to railways, many of them notices of plans for new lines for which bills were being submitted to Parliament before an annual deadline. Someone calculated that the capital needed to fund all of these schemes would be £334 million. The *Mercury* for 23 August 1845 illustrates the mania at its height, announcing three major projects that would have affected the town. The Direct London and Exeter would serve Hammersmith, Hounslow, Staines, Wokingham, Kingsclere and Andover, thence following the route now used by South West Trains. The GW itself proposed a Devonport, Bristol and Dover Railway, which would run from Reading through Farnborough, Guildford, Dorking and Reigate; this was the first hint of the present North Downs line. In another speculative move prompted by the GW's likely extension to Hungerford, the Kennet and Avon Canal Company seriously proposed converting their waterway to a railway. In its favour it was argued that it would avoid the 'obnoxious' Box Tunnel. (Reading's own author Mary Russell Mitford is said to have hired a fly from Chippenham to Bath to avoid it.) A few months later the company thought they might keep the water for goods traffic and build passenger lines along both banks. In September another version of the North Downs line was mooted, this time reaching Dorking by way of Ascot and Leatherhead; within a week the route had changed back to the present one via Guildford. The GW had no part in this scheme. A further 'maniacal' scheme was the Direct Western, diverging from the GW at Reading and passing through Marlborough, Westbury, Wells and Tiverton *en route* to Land's End.

1846   In 1846, after long discussions on the 'Gauge War', Parliament passed an Act under which all new railways were to be built to the standard gauge; but the GW could continue to build branches and connecting lines on the broad gauge. In the company's February report the Chairman said that an extension of the line from Paddington to London Bridge was still under consideration. In June the backers of a London, Newbury and Bath Direct Railway hoped to run west from the GW at Hungerford, noting that 'the double gauge might be laid down'; this anticipates the mixed three-rail track that was to become commonplace on the GW. In September the new bridge over the Oxford Road collapsed; the Council asked the GW to put an ornamental brick balustrade on its replacement. The Berks and Hants lines to Basingstoke and Hungerford were nearly ready in May 1847; the Caversham Road bridge needed widening, and

Crossrail: the way to Essex

Britain's railways were built by competing private companies, and although each line had to obtain an Act of Parliament the government did not impose an overall plan, as happened in France. The railways serving London were about getting people into and out of the capital, not across it; travellers had to use cabs, and later buses and the underground, to get from one terminus to another.

From the earliest days, however, there were schemes – put forward by ingenious individuals rather than railway operators – for cross-town or circular links. In 1845, at the height of the mania, Robert Stephenson proposed a tunnel from Paddington to Shoreditch, where the line would join the Eastern Counties Railway towards Ipswich. The same year brought an idea for an Ipswich and Southampton line, passing well clear of London by way of Braintree, Hertford, High Wycombe and Reading; again, the GW was not involved. In 1851 George Remington, a vigorous proponent of such schemes, suggested a Grand Metropolitan Central station at Smithfield, with links to all the main lines. (This and other such plans are well described in Barker and Hyde's book *London as It Might Have Been*.)

In 1907 a sort of North Circular railway was proposed, running from Feltham to Barking with links to all the radial main lines including the GW at Southall; this was primarily intended to take freight to London docks, but a Reading–Shenfield journey would have been possible. The 1944 Greater London Plan contained the first suggestion of a fast link from Paddington to Liverpool Street, but post-war infrastructure work had to concentrate on repairs rather than new builds. This proto-Crossrail idea resurfaced in a 1974 plan for a link serving Ludgate Hill and Leicester Square, and continuing to Heathrow.

In 1980 Peter Parker, Chairman of the British Railways Board, suggested main line standard links from the Southern Region to the lines out of Euston, St Pancras and King's Cross, with a possible spur from Victoria to Paddington (with no intermediate stations). In 1989 a Paddington–Liverpool Street line was discussed again, and two years later the first version of the current Crossrail scheme was mooted. Initially the only eastern terminus was to be Shenfield; at the other end it would have branches to Reading and Aylesbury. Nothing happened for a while, but by 2003 the western termini were to be Heathrow and Richmond; the following year Maidenhead came into the picture, along with an eastern arm to Ebbsfleet, where a Eurostar station was opened in 2007. This branch was later cut back to Abbey Wood. In 2004 a rival and much more ambitious plan called Superlink briefly emerged, restoring Reading to the map along with Basingstoke; to the east it would go all the way to Ipswich and Cambridge. This idea was rejected in 2005.

In 2000–2002 trains did run from Basingstoke into East Anglia, using existing tracks via Feltham and Acton and the North London Line to Stratford; from Reading one could join this 'London Crosslink' at Staines for a hassle-free but slow and infrequent journey into East London and Essex. Finally, from 2002 to 2008 a Virgin cross-country train from Manchester ran via Reading and Kensington Olympia, not to Essex but to East Croydon and Brighton. This left Reading at 11.12 am; simultaneously two other London-bound trains slid out, bound for Paddington and Waterloo.

The Crossrail now being visibly built just outside Paddington was approved in 2007; work began in 2009, and the first section is scheduled to open in 2015. Now that the GW main line is to be electrified, there is no physical reason not to bring Crossrail to Reading, or indeed beyond to Newbury and Oxford; the distances are comparable with Bedford and Brighton, which have been served by Thameslink since 1988. At the time of writing, Crossrails 2 and 3 are being discussed.

the *Mercury* hoped that it would become 'an ornamental entrance to the town'. The Council agreed.

1848   By 1848 the mania had been damped down by an economic depression. Existing projects plodded on, if not always smoothly, especially on the Reading, Guildford and Reigate line. A bridge under construction near Mr Shackel's farm off the Wokingham Road fell down; the *Mercury* complained about the company's men working on Sundays; and they had yet to decide where to put their station. The townspeople worried that their enjoyment of the Forbury would be impaired. The GW, too, had problems. In May there were complaints about timekeeping (very likely thanks to the one-sidedness of the station) and staff attitudes. Return or day tickets were withdrawn, only to be reinstated six months later. The Basingstoke line opened on 1 November and immediately provoked a complaint: a traveller expected to find the train at the Down station, but was directed to 'another platform, considerably lower down'. This is baffling: was it a temporary arrangement?

1849   The Reigate line was operated from the outset by the SE, reaching well out of their home territory; it is now a First Great Western branch penetrating the domains of Southern and South West Trains. The line dominated the news again in 1849. In March they were still excavating in King's Meadow and diverting the Plummery stream. On 7 July two portions of the line opened, from Reigate to Dorking and Farnborough to Reading, using a temporary one-platform station some way along Forbury Road. The *Mercury* reported that traffic on its four daily trains was 'merely nominal', as it served nowhere significant other than Wokingham. By changing stations at Farnborough (and paying a higher fare than the GW's) you could reach Waterloo in two and a quarter hours, and indeed the SE hoped to build a direct connection onto the main line from Southampton. On 28 July a fete was staged at Luckley Park, Wokingham, and the company showed enterprise by letting people off their trains at the gates. The line opened to Guildford in August, and throughout in October. Six trains a day ran to London Bridge via

Redhill and Croydon, the fastest taking 2 hours 38 minutes. First, second, third and parliamentary fares were available.

1850   By March 1850 the line was carrying a lot of goods traffic to London, thereby achieving Brunel's dream of a direct link to the tidal Thames – but without using his line. The SE continued to show initiative, building a siding at Loddon Bridge for the convenience of anglers, starting to install the electric telegraph, and running an excursion from Reading to Ramsgate. The *Mercury* carried an advert for a school in Tunbridge Wells, claiming that 'railway travelling from Reading is both cheap and expeditious'. There was less than good news for the SE late in the year: the London Road bridge already needed repair, and people complained about the

GW and SE stations, c. 1850

by A Ashley

station area. They had made the roads around the Forbury 'a slough of despond', and erected a series of 'most frightful elevations, destroying all the attractions of this public promenade'.

1851
1851 saw some lobbying: the *Mercury* urged both companies to run cheap trains to the Great Exhibition (they did) and the Mayor wanted the GW to issue season tickets. They complied, but only to Windsor and Maidenhead; after more prompting Reading qualified too. On 22 November an explosion injured a man and tore up part of a platform. Apparently the water pipes used to fill the tenders were heated by gas to prevent freezing; when the flame went out, the staff foolishly investigated with a naked candle.

Going off the rails: crime on the line

Trains have long been associated with various criminal activities, some of them railway-specific. The navvies who built the line were sometimes unruly; perhaps after a long hard day's work they spent too much of their wages on drink. On the trains, before corridors were introduced, a compartment was a convenient venue for assault or murder. More publicly, pushing someone off a platform under a speeding train would mean almost certain death. Reading does not seem to have been a hotspot for such violence, though infanticide is occasionally recorded. In 1850 the body of a female child was left in a parcel at the station 'until called for by Mrs Smith'; no such person appeared, and the truth was revealed after two weeks. A similarly gruesome package was found on a train from Hungerford in 1902. Suicides, successful or attempted, were crimes for many years, and occurred nationwide. Passengers were robbed from time to time. In Reading, the Down platform was a noted haunt of pickpockets, who were naturally assumed to be Londoners. The railway itself was the victim of theft: in 1858 a juvenile was convicted of stealing iron bolts from the Caversham Road works. Fare-dodgers have always been with us, and in the nineteenth century those caught were invariably prosecuted and reported in the local press. Finally, trains made excellent getaway vehicles for all sorts of offenders. One notable and well-prepared forger on the run is said to have joined a lady in a compartment at Paddington; as the train sped westward, he asked her to cut all his hair off and then to look the other way while he changed his clothes. Despite the alarm having been sent ahead by the electric telegraph, the police failed to recognise him at Reading.

1852   From 1852 the SE ran an 08.45 express reaching London Bridge in two hours, which no doubt appealed to leisured businessmen working short hours. It called at Guildford, Shalford and Dorking only. The stop at the small village of Shalford is interesting; perhaps it served as a kiss-and-ride (or tether-and-ride) station, avoiding congestion in the centre of Guildford. In April landowners and residents along this line petitioned the Board of Trade, arguing that it had been built with the promise of through trains off the GW to the Channel ports. This had not happened, and the two companies were deliberately missing connections; furthermore, the SE line did not go into the GW station, necessitating a quarter-mile walk. In October the GW reached Birmingham, with 13 trains a day taking two hours and 35 minutes. In this year George Measom published his *Illustrated Guide to the Great Western Railway*; of Reading he writes:

> This is a first-class station, situated in a siding, covered from end to end, and provided with every convenience for the great traffic of so important a place; but still it is by no means so commodious and well-adapted to its purpose as those at Didcot and Swindon.

This may have been the first complaint in print relating to Brunel's one-sided arrangement.

1853   In February 1853 the SE sought parliamentary powers to extend their line into the GW station, or, failing that, to build their own adjacent to it. A *Mercury* editorial praised the SE line, its scenery, and the delights of Redhill. In August the LSW company secured a Bill for a Staines, Wokingham and Woking Railway, with running powers over the SE into Reading and onto the GW, thereby providing a third route to London.

In a major mishap on 15 October a faulty goods truck passed through the down GW station with a heavy metal flap sticking out sideways; it demolished a number of columns and much of the timber and zinc roof. The *Mercury* commented: 'We are aware that the directors have long contemplated either altering or reconstructing the stations, as they have been found very insufficient and inconvenient ...'. This

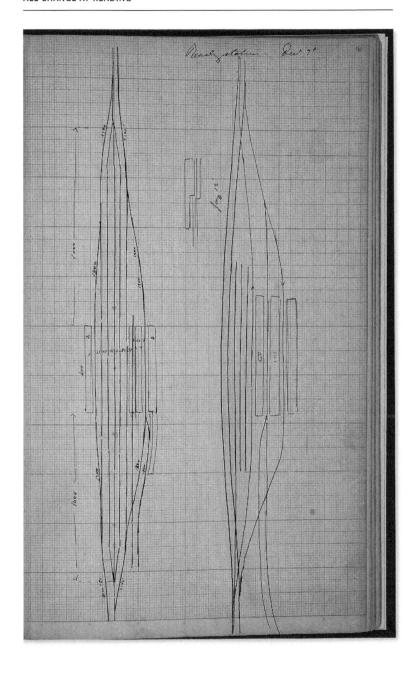

may well have been wishful writing on the paper's part, but probably reflects public dissatisfaction. No such rebuilding happened, of course, but in this year Kit Talbot, a close associate of Brunel, wrote to his cousin W.H. Fox Talbot:

> Did you but know how your life depends on the steadiness of the signalmen at the parts where other railways meet and cross! I said one day to Brunel while we were coming up [to London] 'I am always glad when we have passed the Reading points, they are so complicate[d] ...' I wanted his assurance there was no danger but his reply was 'And so am I'.

1854 So Brunel was aware of a problem, and in December he made sketches showing revised layouts. In August 1854 he wrote to the GW's chairman, C.A. Saunders: 'I do not know on what principle to make estimates of the probable expenditure on stations – for the purposes of obtaining grants – is there to be a special grant for Reading station?'

1855 In 1855 the Council objected to the Staines, Wokingham and Woking proposal because it would cross the Vastern footpath and Caversham Road on the level, endangering lives. The March timetable had 16 trains a day to Paddington, eight each to Bristol and Birmingham, five to Basingstoke and four to Hungerford. The SE ran only four to London Bridge. On 12 May the brick piers to carry the new two-platform SE station were being erected in the meadow adjoining the Great Western Hotel. The old engine house and other buildings near the Forbury were to be removed. Excursions dominated the news in late summer. The SE ran one from London to Reading for the races at a fare of 2s.6d.; the GW followed suit reluctantly, at short notice, and no doubt at a higher price. They did run a trip to Portsmouth, with a change at Basingstoke. A letter complained that

Brunel's drawings of station layouts, probably Reading, 2 December 1853. These show platforms on both sides of the line, but the one-sided station survived into the 1890s. Reproduced by permission of the Brunel Institute, Bristol.

Burrowing into the heart: the Metropolitan connection

Having decided not to bring its line to Waterloo or London Bridge, the GW realised that their terminus was remote from the City of London. In its early years, many coach and omnibus operators ran from Paddington to the Bank of England along the 'New Road' (now the Marylebone and Euston Roads; it was new in 1756 as the world's first bypass, taking livestock to market). There was clearly a demand for some sort of mass rapid transit on this corridor, and several railway schemes were proposed. In 1845 'the project of a metropolitan railway tunnel is beginning to be seriously entertained'. This first plan for an underground would have started at Hyde Park Corner and gone east, with stations at every chief thoroughfare; it evidently was not intended to join any main lines. Another idea put forward in 1853 had trains 'propelled without locomotives'; this probably meant the atmospheric system.

The progenitor of the successful Metropolitan Railway was Charles Pearson, a solicitor. In 1854 he persuaded the GW to invest in his line to Farringdon Street, the world's first urban underground railway. Opened in 1863, it was built with mixed gauge from the start so that the GW could run through from the main line. It used special engines that were supposed to consume their own smoke. One of them was on display at Reading station in 1862; the *Mercury* called it 'a very ponderous machine'. The GW agreed to run the whole intensive Metropolitan operation, but very quickly lost interest (and money) and restricted their participation to trains running through to their own lines. These went out to a number of destinations, notably Windsor, where a public meeting had called for Metropolitan trains as early as 1858. In due course the GW penetrated other parts of inner London: they reached Victoria via the West London line through Kensington Olympia, and Mansion House on the District line. Windsor was as far as the Met trains reached; early timetables suggest that some trains came to Reading, but they were almost certainly connections rather than through services.

excursions from London to the West Country would not pick up passengers at Reading. Another correspondent told of a trip from Wallingford Road (near Cholsey) to Paddington taking four hours to cover 47 miles. The SE ran all the way to Boulogne (but not there and back in a day). And finally, unprecedentedly, the rival companies joined forces with an excursion (or rather a through excursion ticket) from Hungerford to Brighton. In December the GW announced that 'during the hunting season, gentlemen may have their horses forwarded to Swindon by the morning express'. The Town Council now had an active Railway Committee; it pressed for more trains to carry mail, pointing out that post from the Midlands to Reading went via London. (Nowadays letters from one Reading address to another are taken by road to Swindon and back.)

1856   Early in 1856 there were stirrings towards a possible new main station. The *Mercury* confidently reported that the GW had bought a mile-long strip of King's Meadow for additional tracks and an Up station, 'avoiding the crossing to which every train is now subject'. It also mentioned a thoroughfare under the line. Sir Charles Russell, ex-chairman of the GW and Tory MP, shot himself on 15 May. He is said to have championed workers' rights; he also loyally supported Brunel and the broad gauge. On 9 July the LSW began running six trains a day from Reading to Waterloo, in a best time of 114 minutes. The *Mercury* announced in advance that the fares would be 'tolerably moderate', but a week later it admitted that they exceeded the GW's and were nearly double the SE's. Fares were news again in November, when 'the inhabitants of this town have been much amused at the spirit of competition which has existed between the GW and the SE ...'. Prices were cut twice in one day, with all three companies coming down to 1s.3d. to London. In this year the south-to-west curve across Cow Lane was built with mixed gauge, allowing standard gauge trains to run through from the North and the Midlands to the South Coast without reversing at Reading station, which remained wholly broad gauge. The LSW and SE again sought to extend their narrow gauge tracks westwards and obtain running powers to Oxford and beyond; rather than co-operate, they proposed separate routes, crossing the Caversham Road by bridges north and south of the main lines.

1857   The SE's timetable for May 1857 stepped up its service from five to seven trains a day; they boasted that you could now leave Reading in the morning and reach Paris (via Redhill, Tonbridge, Ashford and Folkestone) the same evening, with a through ticket. The GW opened the Henley branch in June; fares were 'ridiculously high' and connections poor, and the first train carried only six people. Fares were belatedly reduced some ten months later. The company's August meeting heard that it was on good terms with other companies – except for the SE. There could soon be a continuous narrow gauge route from the north of England to Folkestone for France 'if the companies worked harmoniously'. A Mr Brown asked 'whether the alteration or rebuilding of Reading station was given up or not?' The Chairman replied that they had no intention to rebuild or alter at present.

1858   In February 1858 the GW finally agreed to build the narrow gauge connection with the SE and LSW lines. In June all three companies agreed to abolish cheap fares. The *Mercury* regretted this move, saying they had been a great benefit to the public, like the penny post. In September the companies made a pact to pool and share all fares to London. In December the SE ran an excursion to Millwall on the Isle of Dogs to enable people to admire Brunel's Great Eastern steamship; by far the largest vessel ever built, it had been launched, with considerable difficulty, in January. The GW–SE narrow gauge link finally opened, by way of the skew underpass (reinstated in 2013) to the east of the station; in March two special military trains used it to bring more than 1000 people from Preston and Bury, Lancashire, to North Camp, Aldershot. *The Daily News*, quoted by the *Mercury*, praised the GW's improved management and dropped another hint of a new station for Reading.

GW Down railway station, 1860

One of the GW stations, c. 1860

1859   In 1859 the GW opened its works on the east side of the Caversham Road 'to execute materials necessary for the repair of the line'; this work had previously been contracted out.

On 26 June disaster struck the SE: their wooden station was entirely destroyed by a fire that started when lightning struck the lamp room, no doubt igniting cans of oil. The station superintendent tried to save money and papers, to little avail. Two staff cottages survived; five horses managed to escape from their stable; the telegraph was knocked out. The GW staff were praised for their help. Remarkably, the SE went ahead with an excursion to Boulogne within a fortnight. Brunel died on 15 September. Though still on the GW payroll, he had for some while been mainly occupied making ships and docks.

1860   By May 1860 the SE were planning a replacement station with four platforms; the *Mercury* regretted that it was not to be combined with the GW's, an arrangement which would be 'much more convenient and perfectly practicable'. In October the GW sought powers to take the narrow gauge into Paddington – and to rebuild Reading station. On 15 December the *Mercury* printed an editorial on the 'battle of the gauges'; rather than looking forward to the abolition of the broad, it saw mixed gauge as the solution.

1861   The new SE station was said to be nearly finished in February 1861: its external appearance was 'substantial and tasteful', the ticket office was already open, refreshments were available, and the stationmaster had an apartment on the first floor. By August the mixed gauge had reached Paddington. At Reading, a new platform and temporary station were to be erected 'beyond the present up-station'. This evidently did not happen.

1862   In January 1862 the employees of the Caversham Road works and their families, totalling 400 people, were entertained to tea. They sang Grace before tucking into 240 lbs of Huntley & Palmers' cake. The manager made a long speech praising the firm's good industrial relations – and

Many a slip: how to get off a moving train

One of the world's odder railway operating practices was the slip coach, invented by the London, Brighton and South Coast company in 1858 and used on various lines for over a century. It enabled fast trains to set down passengers at intermediate places without stopping: on the approach to a station, a guard would uncouple the rear 'slip' coach (or two or three), apply its brakes and bring it to a platform. At junctions the slipped portion might then be attached to a branch train. It sounds dodgy, but there was only ever one serious accident (not on the GW). Slips did, however, have several drawbacks. First, there was no way of reversing the process, attaching coaches to the back of speeding trains, although Wilson and Day's *Unusual Railways* mentions a working model of such a system. Second, it was labour-intensive, requiring two or more guards per train as well as shunters to clear the slips from the platform and re-marshal them into other trains; this made for an unbalanced timetable. Third, people in the slips could not walk through to the dining car.

Slipping was not one of Brunel's ideas, though he made a drawing of a detachable 'slip truck' for use in the construction of the line. But the GW took up the slip coach system rapidly and enthusiastically; from November 1858 they were slipping two portions off a Birmingham train, at Slough and at Banbury. The first slip to serve Reading ran in 1864, but the one-sided station left little room for the necessary manoeuvres. Slips proliferated elsewhere around the GW network, the majority of them from Down trains. In 1884 a man was killed by a slip at Twyford; presumably he had seen the main train pass through and was not expecting another coach to follow so soon. In 1899 a *Railway Magazine* article by J.W. Scott said:

> Should a new coat of arms be adopted by the ancient borough of Reading, we understand that a slip-coach 'proper' (i.e. snuff-brown and cream-white) will form part of the blazon. Certainly no other place in Britain, and therefore, one may take it, in the world, receives 'slips' from so many trains.

The new platforms just opened must indeed have made slipping at Reading a more practical matter. Local people said it was a lot easier to arrive at Reading than to depart. In 1908 the GW was dropping 79 slips a day at 43 locations, representing about half of the national total. Because of demands on manpower during World War I, all slips were suspended for two years. By 1927 Reading had regained four; in the evening rush-hour, Maidenhead enjoyed one and Taplow a generous three. Scott, writing at the turn of the century, tells of 'an exultant Tilehurstian' waiting at Paddington for his slip service: meeting a Reading-bound friend, he boasted 'So sorry we can't travel down together, but, you see, *our* express doesn't stop at any *intermediate* station'. Around this time, many of the fastest station-to-station average speeds were achieved by slip coaches. Most railways abolished the practice in the 1930s, and after another wartime break the GW was the only company to revive them. They continued well into nationalisation days: the last ever, to Bicester North, off a Paddington–Banbury train, ran as late as 1960.

reminding the men of the evils of the demon drink. The afternoon ended with songs. The February half-yearly meeting of the GW heard a Mr Malins boldly urge the abolition of the broad gauge. In March the *Mercury* referred to unspecified 'alterations and improvements recently effected' at the station. In April the LSW decided to cease running excursions on Sundays; the *Mercury* approved. In May the GW built an additional siding and yard near the Caversham Road bridge for cattle traffic. At the end of the month the narrow gauge was being laid from the station to the site of the later Reading West station, so that trains (including royal ones from Windsor) could pass from the London direction to Basingstoke and beyond 'without reversing at Battle Farm'. All three sides of the triangle now had the narrow gauge. In August the GW ran a 22-coach special from London for the Reading races. In the opposite direction a special train from Hungerford taking people to the International Exhibition in London had 2100 passengers on board by the time it reached Reading, where 600 more were waiting. Officials mustered a relief which apparently contained whatever carriages they could find, broad and narrow, providing a rare, if not unique, mixed-gauge train. The GW and LSW announced that they had 'arranged their differences'; the former would avoid Southampton while the latter would not attempt to reach Bristol. A few months later the two companies, along with the London and North Western, made a pact allowing them to use each other's lines 'as far as necessary, to avoid the projection of new ones'. In December the SE proposed to build a new engine shed and convert the old one to a goods warehouse. 'The Forbury Gardens will thereby be greatly benefitted, as the smoke from the engines was often found not to blend very agreeably with the perfume of the flowers', wrote the *Mercury*.

1863   On 31 January 1863, three and a half years after the great fire, the *Mercury* carried an article about the palatial-sounding new SE terminus:

IKB: I Know Best

Isambard Kingdom Brunel, he of the resounding name, has become a posthumous National Treasure. A poll voted him Second Greatest Englishman Ever; a glossy book dubs him 'The Man Who Built Britain'; others go further, crediting him with 'Building the Modern World'; the *London A–Z* lists 22 'Brunel' streets and places. *Chambers Biographical Dictionary* devotes only two lines out of 17 to his railway work and has nothing but praise. The sober *Oxford Dictionary of National Biography* is generally favourable, but does admit that 'not all of his ideas and ventures were successes'.

So what should be history's verdict? On the plus side, no-one could fault his bridges. Starting from Paddington, there is the Wharncliffe viaduct over the river Brent at Hanwell. Then Maidenhead, of course: two thin, horizontal piles of bricks hanging in mid-air. They couldn't possibly support themselves, let alone heavy trains; but Brunel got his sums right, and they did and still do, an example of pure function providing beautiful form. Further out there are Gatehampton and Moulsford: all of these Thames bridges were in due course widened, exactly copying Brunel's designs. Was this out of respect, when iron girders might have been cheaper? Chepstow, Saltash, Clifton and the Cornish wooden viaducts were all masterpieces solving particular problems peculiar to their sites, and in 1857 he sketched a Severn bridge like a double-size Saltash which, had it been built, might have been his most impressive work.

As a surveyor, IKB certainly laid out a brilliant line for the GW, and his achievement is not diminished by the fact that it ran close to recently-completed canals where the levels were already known; but it is arguable that his almost-level 'billiard table' from Paddington to Swindon was not really necessary, and a few gentle gradients between river crossings could have saved a lot of earth-moving and eliminated long cuttings and embankments. The broad gauge did in theory and practice give a steadier ride and slightly higher speeds, but it was very soon clear that all other companies were sticking to the narrow, and in due course the GW were obliged to spend great amounts of money to fall into line with national practice. In the formation of the track, Brunel was again on his own: his longitudinal timber sleepers proved unsatisfactory and had to be replaced by conventional transverse ones. He espoused the 'atmospheric' system – whereby trains were drawn along by a piston in a tube laid between the rails – without sufficient testing. He was not a locomotive engineer, but dictated specifications for a batch of engines that were hopelessly inefficient and hardly lasted two years before Daniel Gooch came on the scene and built the world's best for the time. And yet the current Broad Gauge Society has published a pamphlet saying that Brunel's machines 'proved nearly unworkable with the technology available at the time'. No: the blame lies with IKB, not the technology. Finally, and most relevant to this account, there was his crazy concept of one-sided stations. Reading's lasted longest, and its inconveniences are a running theme in this book.

What was his character? Adrian Vaughan in *Brunel: an engineering biography* quotes a revealing self-assessment in a diary entry from October 1827:

My self-conceit and love of glory vie with each other which shall govern me ... I often do the most silly useless things to attract the attention of those I care nothing about. My self-conceit renders me domineering, intolerant even quarrelsome with those who do not flatter.

He was a perfectionist (in pursuit of his own unshakable ideas of perfection) who had difficulty delegating. In some ways he was of a type with his near contemporary, the architect A.W.N. Pugin: both had French fathers, both were the sort of genius who knew they were right when everyone else knew they were wrong, and both were workaholics who died young. Vaughan relates how he fudged facts, fiddled figures and contradicted his own statements to justify his views and actions, and he drops two quiet bombshells near the end of his book. He was not 'a practical railway operator', and again 'he was no railwayman'.

Within the last two years, very considerable improvements have been effected at this station. The new building lately erected, after being allowed sufficient time to dry thoroughly, is now in the course of completion in its internal decorations and fittings. The central portion in which the ticket or booking offices are situated, has been painted, the walls a light green colour, the pillars in bronze, and the woodwork grained oak, evidently with a master hand, and an artistic eye. Several spring cushioned seats have been placed against the walls for the accommodation of second and third class passengers. The walls of the first class gentlemen's waiting room, are covered with a light satin paper, of a neat and modern pattern, and on the floor is a fine Brussels carpet. The chairs are of oak, with American cloth seats, stuffed with hair. The room is lighted with a two-light chandelier, and is a very elegant and comfortable apartment. The first class ladies' waiting room is very snug and warm, but it is not finished. There is, however, evidently a desire to make ample provision for the comfort and convenience of all classes. The architect is Mr T Brady, who has shown great taste and judgment in his plans. The painter's work has been admirably carried out, under Mr Garrod, the foreman, and the joiners' work under Mr Ellis. But these are not the only improvements we have to mention. Within the period stated, we have noticed a great alteration in that low-lying space of ground, between the station and the Great Western Hotel. From a piece of waste land, it has been metamorphosed into a well-cultivated garden, through the industry and good judgment of Mr Carter, the station superintendent. He has also had planted on the slopes, a quantity of evergreen shrubs; and ere long, the place, which was very lately a public eyesore, will be rendered quite attractive. To Mr Carter, also, the public are indebted for a high and dry footpath, leading from the station into Vastern-Lane, a road which formerly in wet weather was almost impassable and bad at any time.

When the contemplated improvements are carried out at the goods station the SE Railway Company will have a Terminus at Reading which will reflect credit on them and be worthy of the town.

Were London-bound passengers tempted by all this luxury to go to Waterloo or London Bridge rather than Paddington?

In the new spirit of co-operation, trains ran through from the North and the Midlands to the Kent coast; the 06.55 from Manchester, for instance, reached Dover at 18.50, after a 30-minute lunch stop at Reading. But such services ceased in 1866 and did not re-start until 1897. The SE continued to run enterprising excursions, one of which left Reading at 05.30, allowed eight hours in Boulogne, and got its tired passengers home well after midnight. Earley station opened in October. The *Chronicle* gleefully reported that 'on Monday last some excitement was caused by an alarm of fire at the GW station, and many wishes for its uncharitable destruction were expressed'. Perhaps prompted by the SE's splendid new facilities, attention now focused on the GW station. In November the Town Council deplored its 'disgraceful state'; the clerks froze in winter and baked in summer; the upper station had no waiting room, which was 'monstrous'. A week later the Reading Corporation weighed in with a 'memorial' or petition to the GW, itemising the station's inconveniences, discomforts and dangers, and condemning its 'unsightly range of wooden sheds'. In December the Mayor 'had been told by a gentleman connected with the railway that the directors were perfectly well aware what a "dog hole" of a place Reading station was'.

1864   1864 brought a further development on the SE: they opened the line from London Bridge to Charing Cross. The benefit to Reading passengers would have been minimal: coming from London you would travel east for two miles, then turn south, and only at Reigate did you get any nearer to Reading. Near Kennetmouth there is still a milepost 68, being the distance from Charing Cross by this circuitous route. One could thus travel to Waterloo by different routes, diverging at Wokingham. Cannon Street opened in

1866, enabling some Reading trains to penetrate the City of London. Through trains continued to run from Reading to London Bridge until 1965. The attacks on the GW continued. The *Chronicle* printed a letter about the 'dirty, ungainly nature' of the station's structure, and its 'inexplicable arrangements', with 'a pretended distinction between the Up and Down stations'. An editorial referred to 'the worst and most beggarly station that imagination could conceive ... a series of dirty wooden sheds, broken only by two dismal and incommodious booking boxes ... the platform in foul weather is simply a dismal swamp'. People pleaded for a midnight train from Paddington (Windsor had one, but the last to Reading left at 20.10). The town's Grand Jury (a body of high-ranking gentlemen whose main duties were concerned with the assizes) made a presentment against the company about the 'perplexing and dangerous' state of the station, 'long and loudly complained of'. The Inspector of Nuisances weighed in, complaining that the GW and the SE were pouring sewage into the Plummery Ditch, thereby polluting public streams. None of these bodies had any real power to force the company to do anything, but at the end of the year the GW finally sought parliamentary permission to build a new joint station – less than two years after the SE had rebuilt their own.

1865   In February 1865 the *Mercury* reprinted a piece from the *Morning Post* listing four accidents that had occurred within half an hour of Reading in recent weeks; the majority involved goods or parcel trains, and the paper recommended building separate lines for this traffic.

The clock turret of the 1867 GW station

A NEW STATION

1865   In April the GW finally bowed to public pressure: Michael
Lane, Chief Engineer, met the Mayor and others to discuss
plans for rebuilding. A new passenger station would be built
close to the present one, though somewhat nearer to the
town; the goods sheds might be north of the lines or in Mr
Flanagan's meadow, between the railway and Friar Street.
The hot topic for the rest of the year was the removal of the
GW's carriage and wagon works from Paddington, along with
1500 workers. Reading was one possible site, and inevitably
there were objectors: one wrote, 'nobody knows how many
tall black chimneys and endless rows of small tenements
would be needed'. H.J. Simonds was in favour, possibly
because he would sell lots of beer to the workers. Oxford was
considered, and of course the academics were opposed; the
company apparently bought 22 acres of land at Cripley Meadow, west of the station, but then decided that the local clay
was not strong enough to support the sheds. Someone proposed Didcot, 'a dreary spot that really wants a population'.
Reading was finally rejected because there was no land near
or cheap enough, and the works went to Wolverhampton.

November brought good news: preparations for a new
Reading station were being pursued 'with vigour'. Foundations, 26 feet deep, were being dug, with a temporary bridge
over the excavations. The Up station was now approached
by a boarded and partially covered way, but those heading
for the Down had to 'wend their way as best they could
through mud and water'. The *Mercury*'s comments, however,
were upbeat:

> The travelling public who have so long and justly com-
> plained of the defective arrangements for their accom-
> modation ... must experience gratification on witness-
> ing the progress now being made in the works which
> necessarily precede the erection of a new building. The
> operations of the excavators already indicate a depar-
> ture from the plans on which the old offices and sheds
> were constructed, and a glance at the drawings prepared

at Paddington shows that the company intend erecting a station which shall fully meet the requirements of the day, and at the same time form a creditable addition to the public buildings of the borough.

It would be of red brick with white brick facings; cornices, mouldings and columns were to use Bath stone. A central turret would house a gasolier to illuminate the booking office, which would open directly onto the Down platform more than 23 feet wide and 'long enough for all possible purposes'. The stationmaster's apartments and offices were to occupy the first floor; an enlarged refreshment room would be served by a kitchen, scullery and cellar below. Steps from the Down platform would lead to a tunnel to the new Up station (which did not materialise) on the opposite side of the line. A similar way was to be constructed for the transfer of luggage, with hydraulic lifts and a tramway. An overall roof was not planned, but there would be sufficient shelter. Two additional lines would be laid for through expresses. The contractor was Mr Lovett of Wolverhampton, and the works would be supervised by Mr Blackall, manager of the permanent way works. As for the SE, 'we believe they want to widen their line from the present siding which abuts the road to King's Meadow, thus effecting a junction with the GW'; a covered way would link the stations.

By the year's end the excavating work was nearly completed, and men were laying down concrete foundations. 'A tramway communicating with the main line is in course of construction near the up platform, the object being to avoid as far as possible the employment of horse-power in conveying materials to the spot.'

1866 There was little railway news in 1866: the Board of Health, concerned with improving the roads around the stations, commented that 'the SE and GW seemed to mistrust each other'.

1867 A progress report in January 1867 said that the new station had proceeded very slowly, though it was now being roofed in. On the other hand,

Nothing in railway management could be worse than

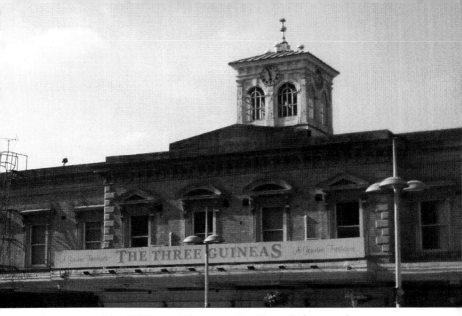

The 1867 GW station, now the Three Guineas pub

the exposed state of the old structure during the late
inclement weather. So wretchedly cold were the offices,
that the ink, we are assured, froze in one of the waiting
rooms.

(No doubt first class passengers were provided with writing
materials.) In February things were looking up; scaffold-
ing was coming down, and 'the building presents a favourable contrast with the old offices'. The new station (now
the Three Guineas pub) is attributed by the new *Pevsner* to
Michael Lane, the GW's Chief Engineer, and described as 'a
nice Italianate job of white Coalbrookdale brick. Pedimented
windows and a clock turret'. In 1975 someone proposed that
it should be a listed building. The Victorian Society declined
to recommend it (was it perhaps not Gothic enough?), but
the Department of the Environment went ahead anyway.
The citation referred to buff bricks and Bath stone dress-
ings. Alan Wykes, writing a few years earlier, claimed that
'no-one could call it architecturally interesting. Still less
could anyone call it attractive.' But he grants that it 'could
... claim to be the most important building in Reading'. At
about the same time Ian House dubbed it 'one of Reading's
best known and least appreciated buildings'. He regretted

the 'gaudy notices along its façade' and the 'bright tin skirt of cars that it always wears'.

1868   In February 1868 the *Mercury* used its regular 'Railway Intelligence' column to reprint an assault on the GW from *The Anti-teapot Review*, 'a magazine of politics, literature and art':

> All sensible people have agreed that the broad gauge, however smooth it may be, is a great commercial mistake, and shareholders have long since felt that Mr Brunel's whims and fancies ought never to have been indulged on a line which was meant to pay good dividends. The GW is a striking exemplification of the 'penny wise and pound foolish' mania which besets some hard-hearted people who ought to know better. On the other hand, the GW has, by its wholesale litigation and extravagant expenditure on useless objects, become the laughing-stock of liberal capitalists.

The anonymous writer went on to criticise the £80,000 spent on Paddington, where 'the public want accommodation rather than decoration'; asks why Reading should be allowed only 'the cold comfort of a few planks (which are absurdly dignified with the title "station") for the shelter of those wretched travellers who, in the depths of winter, are compelled to be *en voyage*'. He also wondered why the last train from Paddington still left as early as 20.10; Windsor enjoyed a midnight departure, allegedly because a GW director lived there.

This was a year of complaints: farmers and dealers wanted better facilities for loading corn at the goods station; and an excursion to Weymouth took six hours outbound and seven and a half back. The unfortunate day tripper commented 'the GW has not lost all its old spirit of making those who travelled cheaply as uncomfortable as possible'. But there was hope in December:

> Travellers have oftentimes experienced great inconvenience owing to several of the Down trains leaving from the Up-station; they will be glad to hear that arrangements have been made, after this week, for all

the Down trains to start from the Lower station. It has also been arranged that all the Up-trains (both broad and narrow gauge) shall leave by the platform adjoining the new Up-station, which will avoid the inconvenience of crossing over the staircase bridge, as has been hitherto necessary for passengers wishing to use the narrow gauge platform.'

It is not clear when this platform was built, but it seems to have been quite short.

1869 Work trundled on through 1869. In August the GW wanted to remove goods and mineral traffic from the passenger station (one wonders why it was there at all). A month later 'alterations and improvements are gradually being made'; large portions of the old woodwork at the old Up station were removed. The public were again assured that all Down and Up trains would now use the appropriate platforms. The new building, 'when finished', would be an ornament to the town. In November Messrs Blackwell of London Street started publishing a monthly pocket timetable for Reading and neighbourhood. The Post Office planned to erect telegraph wires from their premises in Broad Street to the GW goods station via Union Street, Merchants' Place and Hope's Meadow, adjoining the Railway Tap. They soon changed their minds: to avoid ugly posts, even by this back-street route, they went underground.

1870 Huntley & Palmers' new biscuit factory was formally opened in April 1870, but not yet connected to the SE and LSW lines. In June a correspondent complained about smoke from the SE: 'At certain hours of the day, when the wind is in the quarter that has so long prevailed, the Forbury Gardens are literally darkened with a most offensive smoke that issues from the neighbouring goods station'. August brought yet another weary report of 'considerable alterations and improvements' at the GW station. The old engine house was to become a goods shed.

1871 In March 1871 a petition again pleaded for a midnight train from Paddington, but the Town Clerk thought only three people would use it; 22.00 would be more reasonable.

In June the seaside beckoned: Huntley & Palmers took 500 workers to Hastings, and the GW enterprisingly ran through trains thrice weekly to Portishead on the Bristol Channel, connecting with a steamer to Lynmouth and Ilfracombe. Less happily, on 29 July the *Mercury* reported that 'the railway disaster of this week was in Tennessee ...'; accidents, if not disasters, were indeed still quite regular events. In November a meeting of GW staff asked for a 12-hour day, including two hours for lunch, overtime, and extra pay for night and Sunday work. A local branch of the Amalgamated Society of Railway Servants was formed 18 months later.

1872   1872 was a very busy year. Reading finally got its midnight train from London. A Severn Tunnel Bill was put before Parliament, then withdrawn in favour of a bridge. Newbury petitioned for a broad gauge through train to Paddington, avoiding a change at Reading. The National Association pressed for nationalisation and standardised fares, while all the big companies agreed to increase them. The Reading Board of Health wanted better lighting under the Caversham Road bridge. There were more complaints about the SE's 'dense poisonous smoke': engine no. 155 was the worst offender. The coal used 'has a very coke-like appearance, certainly not the smokeless steam coal'. The GW's August report claimed that the policy of carrying third class passengers on all trains had lost them revenue. (The Glasgow and South-Western found the opposite to be true.) At Reading station a man tried to get off a moving train, fell between the coaches and was crushed to death. He was described as 'not in drink'. Nationally, 404 people had died on the railways in 1871; in only 12 cases was the operator declared to be at fault. The transhipment of coal from one gauge to the other was causing delay and inconvenience. The Abingdon branch was converted to narrow gauge after only 16 years of operation.

Mixed gauge track at Didcot Railway Centre

EXPANSION: FOUR TRACKS FROM PADDINGTON

1873   In February 1873 the GW announced that £10,000 was ear-
marked for unspecified works at Reading. They also made
the momentous decision to lay a second pair of tracks
from Paddington to Didcot, a project that took many years
but finally forced the company to build more platforms at
Reading.

The LSW rarely featured in the local press, but in 1874 they
seem to have fallen out with the SE, letting it be known that
they wanted their own station on land opposite the gaol.
This would have been inconveniently far from the main platforms. The Town Council discussed a site for a new Post Office; the Mayor said that when this matter was settled they
should take steps to bring about the completion of the GW
station ('Hear, hear' and laughter in the Council Chamber). A
few days before Christmas the Caversham Road engineering
works were almost totally destroyed by fire; unfortunately
the town water supply was turned off at night and the works
main was inadequate. Four hundred men were thrown out
of work, but the GW immediately promised to rebuild. By
the end of this year almost all of their lines could take the
narrow gauge, leaving a great many engines, trucks and carriages 'quite useless in their present state'.

1875   In July 1875 someone started a road coach service between Reading and Windsor, hoping to attract trade away
from the railway; a similar revival of the public stagecoach,
from Oxford to London via Reading, lasted only two months,
despite the *Mercury*'s recommendation of it as 'a change
from the whirl and noise of the railway'.

1876   In 1876 the GW rebuilt their engine shed – but not, of
course, the passenger station. At the annual dinner of the
combined Oddfellows' lodges, their chairman proposed a
toast to 'the town and trade of Reading'. He said that Reading was centrally situated, and that no town could be better
placed for doing a large trade; he pointed out, however, that
a better bathing place was wanted, that the railway station

was one of the most disgraceful in the south of England, and that the gas was good but of an excellent price (laughter). He believed the drainage would be one of the greatest blessings to the town. The Town Council wearily drew up a petition to the GW about the unsatisfactory condition of the station ... it appeared the railway authorities had no intention of providing better accommodation ... inconvenience and discomfort without parallel between Paddington and Penzance ... danger to life and limb ... Up and Down lines still intersect each other ... large bodies were deaf to complaints ... tradesmen had difficulty reaching the goods depot ... need for a footbridge or subway. Alderman Simonds predicted that the document would go straight into the GW's waste paper basket.

1877   In January 1877 the Grand Jury weighed in again. This time the company deigned to reply, expressing surprise at the mention of danger and claiming that they cared about the public. 'At present there are difficulties to surmount before a complete station can be built ... meanwhile, the down platform covering will be extended and the waiting rooms improved.' The foreman of the jury countered that the narrow end of the Down arrival platform near the water crane was dangerous, especially in wet or frosty weather, and the Up arrival platform had an apparently temporary roof supported by posts that were too close to the trains; people could get jammed. The company retorted, claiming that the posts were seven feet from the platform edge.

1878   In 1878 the town's Medical Officer of Health, commenting on seven cases of smallpox, wrote 'Reading being a great railway centre, we are always liable to have the disease imported'. In May Sir Francis Goldsmid, Reading's MP, was killed at Waterloo station, getting off a train before it had stopped. This prompted the LSW to make all new platforms two feet and six inches above rail level.

1879   A mildly scurrilous book about railway operation was published in 1879 by Beecroft of Reading, splendidly entitled *Ernest Struggle; Or, the Comic Incidents and Anxious Moments in Connection with the Life of a Station Master, by One* *who Endured it*. The author, Hubert A. Simmons, did not work at Reading, but he does relate an incident there. One night there was a crash in the station; someone roused the stationmaster, but he merely leant out of his bedroom window, told the foreman and porters to sort it out, and went back to bed. Simmons invented pseudonyms for places on the 'Great Smash Railway': Reading was 'Jam Junction' and Didcot (which he said was a dirty old barn) 'Puzzle Junction'. Station bookstalls were forbidden to sell the work, so he advertised it on large boards in lineside fields. Another memory of these years is found in Molly Hughes's *A London Child of the 1870s. En route* to holidays in Cornwall, she recalls that 'Reading, the first stop, was great fun for those on the near side. What more cheering than to see distracted people looking for seats when we were definitely full up?' Perhaps the *schadenfreude* arose from the Hughes's own problems at Paddington, where they had had to arrive an hour early to secure a compartment to themselves. More anecdotes from the 1870s can be found in William Vincent's *Seen from the Railway Platform*. The author, who ran the bookstall at Reading, tells us that the morning papers arrived from London at 06.23; a special copy of *The Times* was then forwarded to Wokingham, whence a messenger whisked it to Bearwood, home of John Walter, the paper's proprietor.

1880   Yet another petition was drawn up in February 1880, this time complaining that the GW were the only company to charge express fare for short journeys such as Reading to Paddington. At the company's half-yearly meeting they announced that Slough, another one-sided station, would be getting separate Up and Down platforms; a shareholder asked for similar provision at Reading. Work started on the Didcot, Newbury and Southampton line; it was never a commercial success, but could have been a useful Reading bypass for goods trains. In November Mr Peach, stationmaster at Reading for 15 years, retired. A collection was made, and he was praised for his 'uniform courtesy and attention'. No doubt the travelling public understood that the station's defects were beyond his control.

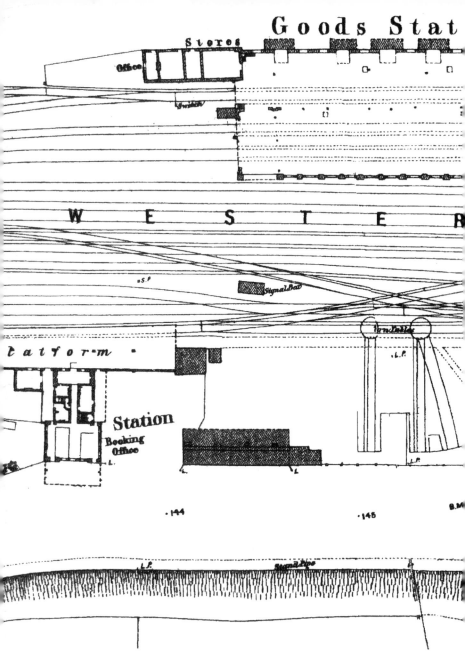

Extract from Ordnance Survey 1:500 map, 1879. On the left is the 1840 Down station; on the right, the 1860s Up station, now the Three Guineas; in the bottom right-hand corner the SW/SE terminus. The trackwork north of the signal box shows how the common rail shared by both gauges changes sides.

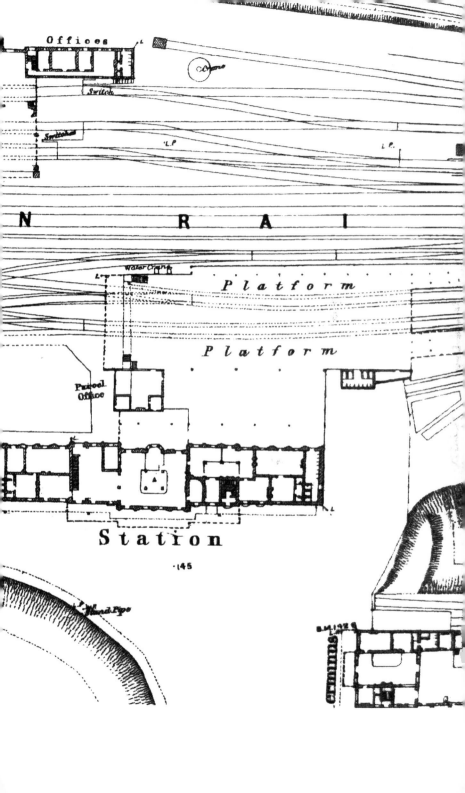

1882   In 1882 the Didcot–Newbury line opened; so did the first station at Tilehurst, a hard, rocky little shelter on platform 1 that would not look out of place in the Highlands. The architect was H.E. Danks, who also did the flamboyant station at Slough. Some years later J.E. Vincent wrote, in *Highways and Byways in Berkshire*:

> Now we are drawing near to Reading. The hills have receded on the left bank; the monotonous embankment of the Great Western Railway, a piece of artificial Berkshire, hides the natural Berkshire from all eyes. Tilehurst (it is true that it is not worth a visit) is almost as far distant as Reading; but Tilehurst station, with extensive platforms and the other appanage of a railway station, is perched close to the river. Why does it exist at all? Did the railway company at any time venture to cherish the hope that upon some future day the vicinity of Tilehurst might blossom forth as a 'riverside resort'? ... Or is it possible that the importance of the station is not entirely disconnected with the presence of an unassuming bungalow across the stream, where the late general manager of the railway, the most genial of men, was wont to make occasional holiday?

This summer the Royal Agricultural Show was staged in King's Meadow, and the railways made considerable efforts to cope with the crowds. Both stations were decorated, and a triumphal arch spanned Station Road; the SE laid temporary sidings and a platform. The GW ran 15 special trains each day of the show, refurnished their waiting rooms, extended the cloak room, repainted the Up and Down buildings, erected a covered way to link them, and even built two extra platforms. One served the Newbury and Basingstoke lines; the other, 600 feet long, stood on the Up side, where a platform could and should have been since 1840. But it was evidently only a temporary affair, and Reading had to wait years more for a sensible layout.

1883   By 1883 the two additional pairs of tracks from Paddington were creeping westward, and the Town Council discussed the GW's plans to take them on to Didcot. A councillor commented, 'that they were going to spend money in widening the line might lead them to hope that some day or other they would spend money improving their station'. (Hear, hear.)

1884 In February 1884 the GW and LSW agreed 'to avoid for ten years at least the foolish contests and the useless and absurd competition of the past, while the traffic of the two companies would be carried on in a manner that would promote the public interest and convenience'. It is not clear what actual changes resulted; a correspondent applauded the agreement but claimed that connections were so bad at Reading that it was quicker to get from parts of Surrey to parts of Hampshire via London. *The Times* approved the ending of inter-company rivalry and noted that staff were to assist in each other's business. It also claimed that the decision had been induced by the great cost of opposing each other's bills for new lines in Parliament.

Slough finally got a handsome and spacious four-platform station. The *Mercury* commented that 'the sheds which have served as a station for so many years will shortly be removed'. Wokingham too was rebuilt this year, but the SE were criticised for failing to abolish the 'dangerous' level crossing (which is still there).

1886 The new Reading gas works opened in 1886, occupying 12 acres at Kennetmouth. High- and low-level sidings were laid in; coal trucks could travel on a viaduct direct to the retort house. The GW experimented with a 'telescopical' axle to solve the gauge problem; but such a device was not perfected until about a century later, when Spanish railways devised mechanisms to change from their wide gauge to standard without stopping.

1887 December 1887 brought yet another plea from the Council for a combined station. The LSW said they had no power to do anything because they had no ownership. The GW agreed that a combined station would be 'no doubt convenient to passengers', but they could not afford it. The SE failed to reply at all; this did not surprise one correspondent, who listed a number of faults including 'the insanitary state of one corner of their Reading station'. He concluded, 'If a company calling itself "Great" refuses to do anything about the station, the matter should be put into the hands of the Railway Commissioners'. Alas, that body was unable to oblige an operator to do anything.

1888   In 1888 the Council decided that a footbridge at Kennetmouth would be a benefit for the public seeking recreation; although the GW, unsurprisingly, refused to pay for it, the Horseshoe Bridge was built three years later. In July there was an exchange of stationmasters. Henry Larkham went to Birmingham Snow Hill, taking a pay cut from £230 to £220 a year. Three months later he was declared bankrupt with debts of £1340, blamed on ill health and gambling. His replacement from Birmingham was a Mr Noble, variously referred to as Charles or William. After three years he was promoted to Bristol and replaced by Mr Fraser from Windsor.

1889   There were encouraging signs of activity in June 1889: 'a large number of workmen have been engaged in making various alterations on the line near the down station. The platform has been considerably extended'. Six months later the *Mercury* was hopeful. After a preamble reciting all the usual complaints, it noted that the quadrupling of the lines had forced the GW's hand; two sets of plans had been made and dropped; and F.G. Saunders of Caversham Grove and C.T. Murdoch, MP for Reading, had joined the Board of Directors. The current plan would have four main lines and a high-level siding branch to connect the three companies' tracks, mainly for goods; and, most importantly, there would be a new Up station building on the north side, reached by a footbridge. The goods yard and depot were to move eastwards.

Towards the end of the year tragedy struck on the SE: John Carter, stationmaster for 30 years, was killed, falling under a train on his own tracks.

1890   Early in 1890 the *Mercury* started a new campaign, for an additional station 'at the west end of town'. This would presumably be somewhere near Scours Lane. The GW and the Council discussed the rebuilding of the Vastern Road bridge, agreeing to a single span of 40 feet. Someone worried that if the walls were lined with white glazed bricks, the intense reflected light would frighten horses. On the other side of town, the GW invited tenders to widen the bridge at Cow Lane. In August the *Mercury* published a review of 50 years of railway development by Arthur Irwin Dasent of Ascot. He lambasted the GW for their inaction over the station, of course, but also criticised them and the LSW on the subject of speed, pointing out that many trains were no faster than in the 1850s.

Broad Gauge locomotive on mixed gauge track at Didcot Railway Centre

THE END OF THE BROAD GAUGE

1891   In March 1891 the *Mercury* considered the imminent final
conversion to narrow gauge. 'Many will hear with regret that
in about 18 months' time the comfortable, smooth running
broad gauge carriages will pass out of use'. By April some
300–400 men were at work widening Sonning cutting and
the embankment on towards Reading. An anonymous correspondent wrote to the *Mercury* in July, enclosing an account
by 'a gentleman who has apparently just seen the Reading
railway station for the first time'. He relates

> the impression left on his mind by the fearful and won-
> derful traffic arrangements at that spot ... every up
> train stopping there has to cross the path of every down
> train, including the expresses on the down line, which
> dash through without stopping. The same murderous
> plan was in operation at Slough until within the last few
> years ... that it should have been carried on without a
> gigantic disaster is indeed a monument to the skill and
> vigilance of the company's servants.

1892   In February 1892 the GW were trying to buy land on the
west side of Station Road, in the occupation of Mr Flanagan, 'apparently to gain access to an approach subway to
their proposed Up platform'. Over a single weekend in May
the broad gauge was finally eliminated as 177 miles of track
between Exeter and Truro were converted by 4000 men
brought by special trains from all over the country. Four
hundred and fourteen of them went down from Reading to
Launceston on the Thursday and came back on the Tues-
day. In September *The Builder* magazine considered the GW.
After praising various improvements on the system it opined:
'It is very strange, however, that the building of a new station at Reading is not taken in hand. ... the elongated shed
which is dignified by the name of a station is inconvenient
and altogether unworthy of an important town'. In October the *Mercury* turned its guns on the SE and the 'totally
inadequate provision for the safety and convenience of passengers. During the recent hop-picking season, it was a mir-

acle that no accident happened.' (Evidently they were running special trains from Reading to the Kentish hop fields.) Turning yet again to the GW, it reported a rumour that the company had abandoned their scheme of a new station in favour of Bath and Cheltenham because Reading people were not sufficiently urgent in pressing for improvements. In November Sir Charles Russell of the SE agreed with the Mayor on the need for a joint station; it was not worth spending money on separate ones. The *Mercury*'s review of the year was upbeat: 'There is now every prospect of a joint station worthy of the town in the immediate future'.

1893   By June 1893 the quadruple tracks had finally reached Reading, and much work had been done further west. Someone complained about the new 15-foot brick wall 'of a hideous colour' by the Thames near Tilehurst – 'a disgraceful piece of vandalism'. Someone else suggested growing Virginia creeper on it.

1894   The most promising signs of potential action appeared in April 1894, when the GW invited tenders to widen two bridges and construct a new bridge and subway and other works 'near the Reading station'. In July they wanted firms to build a shunter's cabin and two cart weighbridges, and in August allocated £50,000 for a new goods shed and siding. The *Mercury*'s end-of-year review was despondent:

> All hope of a joint station has been abandoned, the question of gradients and other matters having presented difficulties which were considered insuperable. A new girder for carrying the widened GW is being pushed on. The SE have submitted plans for an improved station.

These plans did not please the Council, and clearly relations with the GW remained poor.

1895   The SE were still in the news in June 1895: Crowthorne and Sandhurst Parish Councils were pleading for a link onto the LSW at Frimley, which would shorten the route to London by 20 miles. The SE said this would not be in their shareholders' interests – in other words, the company would lose revenue. Instead, in a remarkable piece of timetabling, they

GW station, c.1894

put on a train leaving Reading at 09.55, calling only at Crow-thorne (then named Wellington College) and North Camp before running non-stop to Cannon Street in 104 minutes end-to-end. In a move that provided faster journeys for thousands of GW passengers daily, the company finally paid an astonishing £100,000 to the monopolist caterer at Swindon to release them from the obligation to stop all trains there for ten minutes. Inter-company squabbles continued: in negotiations about a joint station, the Council accused the SE of using the LSW as 'a king of bogey, stopping them doing things'. Alderman Blackall Simonds said it was no use barking if you couldn't bite. By November the GW had rebuilt their side of the Vastern Road bridge; the SE were still dithering and even considering retreating to their original site further east. In a late mini-mania, someone proposed an entirely new London–Oxford–South Wales railway, costing £5–6 million; nothing came of it, but the GW were moved to put on a non-stop run to Newport. Made possible by the installation of water troughs between the rails from which engines could refill at speed, this was thought to be the longest non-stop run in the world. This train was but one of many expresses that did not serve Reading.

Caversham Road Bridge

MORE PLATFORMS AT LAST

1896   1896 was a momentous year: things really began to happen, albeit slowly, on the ground. In June the GW announced
that the erection of a new goods shed east of Vastern Road,
twice the size of the old one, would enable them to clear the
site for their 'grand new passenger station'. (In the event the
new buildings could hardly be called 'grand'.) In August new
platform walls by the Basingstoke and Newbury platforms
were going up; in September the new station plans were on
view for potential contractors. In this year the SE removed
the overall roof from their station.

1897   March 1897 saw riveters working on the Caversham Road
bridge; passers-by complained of being showered with hot
water, cold water and red-hot bolts of fire. In July the GW
and SE collaborated (for once) in a new continental service:
you could leave Birkenhead at 08.57 and travel via Reading
(13.21) to Folkestone, reaching Paris at about 23.00. Such
trains continued until 1917. Before the end of the year the
SE were at last rebuilding their part of the Vastern Road
bridge, and 'considerable progress' had been made with the
new GW station.

1898   'Active progress' was the report in April 1898. On the south
side, a long new range extended the old building, while to
the north the new Up station, with a very long platform,
was to open on 1 May, 45 years after the first complaint
about its absence. They would be linked by a 'capacious and
well-constructed subway' (the one that closed in 1989 and
reopened as a public route in 2013). It was claimed that delays had been reduced by 80 per cent.

1899   The *Bury and Norwich Post* for 7 February 1899 reported a
fire at Reading station, 'a fine building nearing completion'.
It started in WH Smith's, and several offices were damaged.
In June *The Railway Magazine* carried an article by W.J. Scott
about the station and its train services. 'The Great Western
has never been a line of great stations', it began, going on
to praise Paddington and Bristol as the only exceptions. 'It
used, however, to hold a bad pre-eminence in stations which

were at once hideous, inconvenient to the public, and awkward (not to say dangerous) to work.' It then lists most of Brunel's one-sided efforts (without naming, let alone blaming, the great man), dubbing them all 'wooden structures, gloomy, grimy and ramshackle'. Most had been replaced, but

> Reading – the most 'dowie den' of them all – has lingered on to the last years of the century. ['Dowie' is a Scots word for 'dismal'.] True, over thirty years ago improvements were made, and it began to be rebuilt a decade or more ago, but mostly in the Irish way of *pulling down* – the outcome being a 'temporary' Down platform, with rough wooden posts and a roofing of tarred felt. Later on, however, some very satisfactory booking-offices and waiting-rooms in white brick, with a clock-tower, were reared on the Down side, but in the section used as the 'Up station' (for there were no platforms on the proper Up side): these buildings have been worked into the new structure, and form the chief booking-hall, opening onto the No.1 (or Down relief and branch-terminal) platform.

Scott goes on to list the various passenger and goods services that justified so many new platforms. Turning to the station's public face, he suggests that if it had been distant from the town centre, like Didcot, 'its outside elevations and booking-office accommodation might have been on a much smaller scale'. He waxes lyrical over the West Junction signal box, the largest on the GW: the lower storey 'looks like the inside of a giant organ', while above 'the signalman and his telegraph boys dwell in a kind of glass palace, 100 feet long, fitted with all that makes for the comfort of its occupants'.

He then describes the new layout. There were four long through platforms – the present nos. 7–10 – with non-platform through lines between 7 & 8 and 9 &10 which could be used by non-stopping expresses (of which there were still many) or for moving engines from one end of a train to the other when reversing, especially on trains from Oxford and the North to Basingstoke and the South. For services starting and terminating at Reading there were six bay or dead-end platforms: the present 1–3 facing west, two between 8 & 9, one facing each way, and one facing east beyond no. 10, now part of the through platform 11. The new platform buildings were modest red and blue brick efforts, very similar to those still in use at Pangbourne, Cholsey and elsewhere. All of this was done on a budget of £6000, which the GW could surely have afforded many years earlier. Scott spends some time regretting that the company chose not to have overall roofs: he thought that the 'verandah' or 'tin umbrella' awnings gave insufficient protection from the weather. Scott analysed the current train services: he counted 53 on the GW (Down), 14 on the SE (including 11 still going all the way to Charing Cross), and 13 on the LSW.

Rails in Fobney Street at the end of the Coley branch

NEW ROUTES TO THE WEST AND NORTH

So Reading entered the new century with a vastly more convenient station that would serve for 90 years with few major changes or events. In the first decade the GW was busy building shortcuts to the West Country, South Wales and the Midlands; Paddington–Birmingham trains were diverted via High Wycombe. Reading West was put up in 1906 specifically for long-distance north–south trains, to avoid reversal at Reading; it still has much longer platforms than you would expect at a suburban halt.

1908   In 1908 the Coley branch, from Southcote Junction to Reading Central Goods Station, was built, partly to serve lineside industries such as the Co-op jam factory and the Fobney Street maltings, partly to relieve congestion at the main goods yard. Most of the route is now a delightful footpath, and some rails remain embedded in the road by the former maltings.

SW and SE railway station, 1910

GW station, 1926: arrival of the Prince of Wales

1913   An article on 'Reading as a Railway Centre' by H.M. Alderman in *The Railway Magazine* in 1913 surveyed the train services on offer, claiming that 'over 200 commercial travellers who live within the Borough have chosen the town as being ideal from the "Bradshaw" point of view'.

1919   In 1919 T.E. Lawrence (of Arabia) left the sole manuscript of *Seven Pillars of Wisdom* on the station. It was never recovered, and he had to write the book again from memory.

1923   In 1923 most British railways were merged or 'grouped' into four large companies. The GW survived almost unchanged and was the only one to retain the 'Great'; the SE, which already had a 'working union' with the London, Chatham and Dover, became part of the Southern Railway, as did the LSW.

1925   1925 saw the publication of the first edition of *Bacon's Reading and Thames Valley ABC Railway Guide*, listing times and fares for many destinations.

1930   The GW rebuilt their engine shed in 1930. The 1931 Ordnance Survey map shows a number of features, many of them long gone: a weighbridge, a banana ripening shed (built for Fyffes in 1906), hydraulic towers to power the lifts, some lines labelled 'Dunquerque sidings', and other spots known (to railwaymen only) as Top End, Old Bank, and Pugshole. Squeezed between the Southern and GW stations were some allotment gardens, very likely tended by railway staff in their time off. Further out, between the lines at Southcote Junction, stood a pump that presumably sent water from the Holy Brook to the station. On 18 May a touching scene was enacted at the station: the actress Mary Pickford, 'America's sweetheart', was reunited with her second husband Douglas Fairbanks after a four-month separation.

1932   In 1932 the Southern Railway started a programme of electrification on the third-rail 750-volt DC system: Redhill–Reigate first, and Guildford–Ash and Waterloo–Reading in 1939. Reigate–Guildford and Ash–Wokingham were never electrified, though in 1969 British Railways proposed to do so within ten years, along with Redhill–Tonbridge. A photograph in Reading Museum shows a train with a headboard on the front of the engine announcing 'excursion to Huntley and Palmer's, Reading'.

1938   The Oxford Road bridge was rebuilt in 1938.

1939   World War II impinged on Reading in September 1939 when the first consignment of refugees from London arrived from Vauxhall.

1940   In 1940 Reading suffered bombing raids that may well have been aimed at the station; more followed in 1943.

1942   In December 1942 a small ad in the *Mercury* read 'Wanted, Home for Baby, Boy age 1 month; complete surrender'. The child, whose mother could not afford to keep him, was David Sharp, older brother of the novelist Ian McEwan; he was handed over to his adopters on platform 4. The brothers were eventually reunited in 2002.

1947   Nationalisation in 1947 had little effect on day-to-day railway operation. The GW station was called Reading General from 1945 to 1965. It was renamed plain Reading in 1949, and the Southern Region (ex Southern Railway) one became Reading South; but this was changed to Reading Southern in 1961, probably because people might otherwise expect it to be to the south of the town.

The Beeching Axe and the Serpell Scythe

If asked to name two major figures in British railway history, many people would volunteer two Bs: good guy Isambard Kingdom Brunel and bad guy Dr Richard Beeching. In this book I have written some hard things about the former; and while the latter did wield his hugely unpopular axe, leaving some rural parts of the country rail-less, other areas escaped lightly. Beeching's report, carefully entitled 'Reshaping [not Decimating or Devastating] Britain's Railways', appeared in March 1963. Aiming to stop the system losing so much money, it gave examples of lines on which the average train carried passengers in single figures, with huge subsidies per person-mile. Nationally, he closed about 30 per cent of the system (though it should be noted that the Treasury had wanted to lop 70 per cent in 1961). But in this populous and prosperous corner of Southeast England his impact was minimal. The Abingdon branch and the hopelessly uneconomic Didcot–Newbury–Winchester line were already slated for closure pre-Beeching; the report's only local recommendations were the withdrawal of stopping trains and closure of minor stations between Guildford and Redhill, Reading and Westbury, and Didcot and Swindon. Only the last of these threats was carried out; and there is a possibility that a station may reopen at Grove, serving Wantage. The Faringdon, Lambourn and Wallingford branches were not on the axe list and survived until 1972, 1973 and 1981 respectively.

Less well-known is another report published two years later and dubbed Beeching II. Again it had a non-negative title, 'The Development of the Major Railway Trunk Routes', and stressed that its purpose was not to select lines for closure. Looking forward to 1985, it sought to eliminate duplication of main lines and concentrate traffic on selected corridors so as to reduce unit costs. 'Development' was not defined: there were no promises of electrification, resignalling or laying extra tracks. It said almost nothing about the fate of the retained secondary routes: if not to be closed, would they be downgraded to Light Railways, or reduced from double to single lines? Would their unit costs not rise? In the Western Region, Devon and Cornwall were to be served via Swindon and Bristol, not Newbury and Westbury, reverting to the early GW route; Basingstoke–Exeter was also to be de-trunked. But Birmingham–Reading–Guildford–Redhill was selected as part of a London bypass, mainly for freight, from the Midlands to the Channel ports and the proposed tunnel. Surprisingly, Reading–Southampton was expected to attract few passengers; traffic forecasts were generally pessimistic. In the event, the Newbury and Basingstoke ways to Exeter both went on to thrive, as did cross-country trains from Bournemouth to the North. The North Downs line never became a major route to Kent or France but survives to serve both Gatwick and a healthy amount of local traffic.

By 1982 Beeching II's low forecasts of passenger numbers had been proved more or less right, and Margaret Thatcher appointed a committee under Sir David Serpell to consider the railways' future yet again (looking only ten years ahead this time) and to suggest ways of tackling the ongoing losses. The resulting report was not taken up by the government and did not lead to closures or changes, but it is instructive to examine the most drastic (and profitable) of its six options. This would have left the country with a network – hardly that – of just three main lines from London: west, to Bristol and Cardiff, and north, to Scotland by the West Coast and to Newcastle by the East Coast route. One might speculate that if Serpell's ridership estimates had been even lower the GW line might have gone too, leaving only a single Y-shaped line to the Midlands and the North, not dissimilar to the proposed High Speed Two. In the event, passenger numbers rose steadily for the next 30 and more years, and routes that Beeching II had reduced to a single track (Swindon–Gloucester, Oxford–Worcester, Salisbury–Exeter) have in recent years regained a considerable mileage of double track, enabling more frequent and reliable services.

The closure of Reading station is now inconceivable; the last remaining threat to its existence was posed by a very small pressure group called the Railway Conversion League. Their big idea was to rip up all tracks nationwide and lay tarmac for road vehicles, but they never explained how you would fit a motorway into Box Tunnel. The RCL folded in 1994.

1954 The signal works were rebuilt in 1954. In the same year a national modernisation plan started the process of replacing steam engines with diesels and electrics, improving stations and resignalling lines.

1957 On 3 October 1957 a special train full of railway enthusiasts formed a rare passenger service over the Coley branch.

In 1960 expenditure of £2.5 million was allocated to Reading, some of it for improvements to platform 4, including strengthening the roof of the subway. This year saw the introduction of luxury Blue Pullman diesel trains; they served Bristol, South Wales and Oxford, but never stopped at Reading. They were withdrawn in 1973.

1964 From 1964 the Reading–Redhill–Tonbridge service was worked by curious hybrid trains which earned the nickname 'tadpoles'; they consisted of one coach of normal proportions and two thin, flat-sided ones that had been specially built for the Hastings line, which had several narrow tunnels. The tadpoles were scrapped between 1979 and 1982.

1965 In 1965 colour light signals were introduced and the steam engine shed closed. Reading Southern was abolished, its four platforms replaced by the single no. 4a tacked onto the main station; 4b followed ten years later.

1966 The southern part of the Vastern Road bridge came down in 1966.

1967 1967 brought the first of several proposals for rebuilding the station; this one put forward an 'airport-style' edifice.

1968 Reading won the Western Region Best Kept Station Award in 1968, but a year later it needed a task force to clean soot and grime off the walls. As the Channel Tunnel project was revived, there was some talk of trains from the mainland coming through to Reading.

1974 The northern part of the Vastern Road bridge was rebuilt in 1974, and another station plan emerged, this time costing £1.5 million. The first proposal for a Channel Tunnel rail link was published: it would have come through Croydon and over the Thames to a station at White City, where there would have been an opportunity to run trains onto the

Get me to the plane on time: destination Heathrow

Gatwick Airport, sitting on the main London–Brighton line, has had a station since 1935. At Heathrow, on the other hand, the terminals were over two miles from any railway, and the airport relied on road access for many years. Not until 1975 was the Piccadilly line extended from Hounslow, and even then the trains stopped at all stations. The airport had to wait until 1998 to enjoy a fast service, Heathrow Express, running non-stop from Paddington at premium fares. This brought overhead electrification to the former GW territory for the first time. In 2005 a slower, better integrated (but not much cheaper) service branded Heathrow Connect was introduced, allowing access from the west by changing at Hayes & Harlington. But the first dedicated public transport from this direction was a British Railways bus service from Slough, introduced in 1965; the following year it ran direct from Reading under the brand name 'Railair'.

The first suggestion of a direct rail link came in 1997: to be known as 'Airtrack', it was to have opened by 2002. It was back on the agenda in 1999: a route via Staines could be built for £170 million by 2006. The scheme resurfaced in 2003, this time to run to Terminal 5. More recent proposals, with a faster link onto the GW main line near Langley or West Drayton, have yet to be implemented. With or without through trains from the Southwest and South Wales, there is much traffic to be won from road coaches, many of which now serve London's airports rather than the centre of the city.

The commuter's tale, or the Twyford twitch

For more than a score of annual season tickets I travelled nearly a third of a million miles shuttling to and from Paddington. It will be little comfort to patrons of today's crowded rush-hour trains to hear that in the 1970s and 80s commuting from Reading was really not too painful. We had non-stop trains every few minutes running at 90 or 125 mph, many with a buffet car or trolley. Novices soon picked up a few basic knots and wrinkles: learn where to stand on the platform to be next to a door; if things are running out of order, let the first packed train go and find a seat on the next; don't hesitate to occupy vacant reserved seats, as many businesspeople reserve them but don't turn up; likewise, claim seats occupied by luggage (the bigger the bag, the more deserving of turfing out); know that not all trains from the old reversible platform 5 went east to Paddington. Most importantly, scrutinise the national timetable and make a list of the 'secret stoppers' in the evening rush: trains that called at Reading to pick up passengers only and were advertised at Paddington as first stop Newport or Exeter. The rule was unenforceable, no misdemeanour was committed, and the system worked well: the trains were comfortably full until Reading, where we vacated our seats for outer commuters heading westwards from their jobs in Reading. There was one evening, however, when some disruption or incident meant that trains were not what they seemed. An on-train announcement told us that what we thought was the 17.30 to Exeter was a different, re-scheduled 17.30 which really wasn't going to stop before Taunton. It didn't quite get to a whip-round; a deputation found the conductor and he was persuaded to alert the driver. (Nowadays there are no secrets.) For a while there were two trains to Banbury leaving simultaneously at 17.15, one via Reading and one via High Wycombe. I once leapt onto the wrong one and had a slow bus-ride home across the Chilterns. And the Twyford twitch? When the line was quadrupled in the 1890s, the old straight main line became the slow or relief line, and the new fast line had to execute a reverse curve through the station. At 125 mph one felt a distinct lurch to the left and right which conveniently woke us up in time to get off at Reading.

Western main line. These might have included 'Nightstar' sleeping car trains to Cardiff and Plymouth, which could have called at Reading.

1975 In 1975 a new parcel depot went up, and Motorail car-carrying holiday trains started running to St Austell in Cornwall. A prototype gas turbine Advanced Passenger Train with tilting mechanism passed through Reading this year; because of various technical problems the project was abandoned.

1976 From 1976 locomotive-hauled diesel trains were replaced by InterCity 125s. These highly successful and long-lived workhorses are probably now the only trains in the country to retain slam doors – and the prohibition on flushing in stations.

1979 A 1979 rebuilding plan brought the potential cost up to £3 million. In this year the first through trains ran to Gatwick Airport; there were only two a day, travelling via Kensington Olympia and Croydon. More cross-country trains were put on: five a day to Poole and 13 to Birmingham.

1980 From May 1980 a more direct and regular service ran to Gatwick with only three intermediate stops. The *Chronicle* reported that on its maiden voyage it 'sped through Guildford and Redhill'. (The latter feat would have been difficult, as the train had to reverse there.) Another version of the station rebuild plan had added escalators. As in the 1967 proposal, the architect apparently wanted it to feel like an airport terminal; the Civic Society thought that a 'Heathrow Revival' style would remind passengers of the discomforts of air travel.

1981 In 1981 came suggestions for additional suburban stations at Ford's Farm, Calcot, Sutton's Seeds, Church Road Earley, Bullbrook, Emmbrook and Loddon Bridge. Only the last was built, as Winnersh Triangle, in 1986. For a few years in the 1980s a sleeper train ran from Southampton to Edinburgh, picking up at Reading.

1984 The signal works finally closed in 1984.

1988 Another new station, at Thames Valley Park, was proposed in 1988; it has yet to happen. The town's MPs lobbied for a Channel Tunnel freight terminal; the Chamber of Commerce said it would make Reading 'the industrial capital of Europe'. The Oxford Road bridge was beautified with some blue painted doves.

1989   A substantial rebuild, opened by the Queen in 1989, brought a new glass-roofed concourse and the Brunel retail arcade, described by the *Pevsner Architectural Guide* as 'an ungainly extension'. A strikingly tall glass artwork by Alexander Beleschenko was set up in the arcade at a cost of £60,000, but First Great Western controversially scrapped it after ten years; Marks & Spencer now marks the spot. There was also a wide footbridge to supplement the subway, lifts and escalators, and a very big car park. These improvements, it was claimed, 'should see the station well into next century'. The project was about passenger convenience; the rails and platforms were unchanged. Some time later the management decided to install ticket gates; to maintain free access across the station, a fence had to be built on the stairs and footbridge to separate ticketed passengers from the non-travelling public. The 1860s booking office (minus the eastern one-storey wing) became a pub, the Three Guineas. The name refers to a prize in a competition staged in 1904: the GW had decided to put on a new non-stop train to Plymouth and invited the public to suggest a name for it. The winner came up with *The Riviera Express*, though in the event the train was called *The Cornish Riviera Express*. The pub reopened after refurbishment on 1 August 2013. On the walls are a set of GW posters and some arty black-and-white photos of locomotive details.

1991   A new depot for Thames Turbo trains opened in 1991.

1993   On 23 October 1993 an IRA bomb exploded by a signal post just east of the station; Semtex was found in the toilets. This year saw the inception of the Conservative government's railway privatisation programme. It was almost completed by 1997, when Labour regained power; they did not fulfil their pledge to renationalise.

1995   From 1995 you could buy Eurostar tickets at the station.

1996   Berkshire County Council commissioned a study in 1996

The 1989 concourse roof

The going rate: the pursuit of speed

The invention of railways meant vastly quicker journeys for those who could afford them, and until motor cars were widely affordable there was no other way to go. There was, of course, competition between railway operators, and there is evidence that the GW tried harder for the trade to Birmingham (against the London and North Western) and Exeter (against the London and South Western). Their monopoly routes to Bristol and South Wales, arguably, could have been faster.

Trains have, of course, got faster over the years; but for various reasons some have gained speed more slowly than others. Over the almost straight 'billiard table' between Paddington and Reading, a test train just before the station opened in 1840 ran the 36 miles in 45 minutes, and in 1847 a special non-stop made the trip in 37. In commercial service, however, it took 73 minutes or more, thanks largely to a number of intermediate stops. By 1865 this had come down to 47, but only three more minutes were shaved off by 1900. In 1912, 42 minutes was achieved, and 40 in 1927. Post-war, 42 was again the norm, and not until dieselisation did substantial improvements kick in; 1963 brought a 35-minute timing. From 1976 High Speed Trains (HSTs), aka InterCity 125s, famously clocked a standard 22 minutes, and in 1997 a few of them were allowed only 21. A local timetable for that year actually shows a single train allegedly doing the journey in just 20 minutes, averaging a remarkable 108mph, but this may well be a misprint. Since then, sheer congestion (mainly owing to Heathrow Express using the main lines between Paddington and Hayes) has pushed the figure back up to a standard 27.

Turning to London–Bristol, the line's original *raison d'être*, the starting figure was 175 minutes. In 1841 Brunel wanted to demonstrate that he could do it in a flat two hours (if he tried, he evidently failed). Several times the management promised a regular service at this speed, but in 1865 the best timing was still 160 minutes, and in 1887 it was 164. At the turn of the century it was down to 132 minutes, but wartime slowed it to 152. The flat two hours had been achieved by 1933, with another 15 minutes lopped off two years later. In 1952 it had slipped up to 140, but by 1959 a record 94 minutes had been made by a diesel. A special non-stop test run in 1984, undoubtedly using the shorter and straighter route via Bristol Parkway, achieved an amazing 62 minutes. The regular time now is 99; the new trains to be built under the Inter-city Express Programme (IEP) to replace the HSTs should be capable of 69 minutes non-stop via Parkway and 75, with five stops, via Bath.

Finally, Waterloo–Reading. When the line opened in 1856 this journey took 114 minutes. By 1888 it was down to 85, but from 1900 to 1933 it varied between 90 and 100 minutes. Electrification took it down to 75, and little has changed since then except for a brief season in 1971 when some trains with limited stops covered the distance in a record 64 minutes. The current figure, 80 minutes, could be substantially reduced if the service were increased to four per hour (as it was between 2001 and 2003), two of which could be semi-fast.

that recommended new stations at Burghfield Road, Graze-
ley, the Madejski Stadium and Thames Valley Park.

1997–
1999
A very grand scheme was floated by the MEP for the Thames
Valley in 1997. Using hypothetical EU money, Eurostar could
reach Reading within five years, perhaps with a new terminal at Thames Valley Park. France would be a mere two
hours away. Railtrack announced a modest rebuilding plan
in 1998: £8 million would buy two new platforms and reopen the skew dive-under to the east. In 1999 the Prudential
supported a station at Green Park to serve their proposed
development. Planning permission was given in 2001.

2000
The 2000 version of a new main station, a two-tier affair,
put the cost up to £250 million. The job would be done in
2005–7, and there might be temporary 'parkway' stations to
the east and west of the main site.

2002
Virgin Trains, who then had the cross-country franchise,
introduced new trains and an enhanced timetable in 2002.
Branded 'Operation Princess' and presented as a 'new
dawn', it boasted a half-hourly core service from Reading to
Birmingham, with through trains to Scotland and the South
coast. The dawn faded somewhat as some destinations
dropped off the network: once again you had to change to
get to Liverpool, Glasgow, Portsmouth or Brighton. Most
trains going north head for Manchester or Newcastle, with
a solitary extension to Edinburgh; to the south it's all Bournemouth except for one that spends the night at Guildford.
Some of the 'Voyager' units on these services had a tilting
mechanism to enable them to run faster round curves, but
this has not been used for some while.

2003
In 2003 the Strategic Rail Authority hinted at a capacity
upgrade for Reading, which might start in 2008.

2004
After 160 years, the last mail train ran from Reading in
2004.

2005
In 2005 Reading was reported as having the worst delays
in the country, with 25 per cent of trains running late. Yet
another rebuilding plan would have provided two additional
platforms, costing a mere £68 million.

View of the main entrance escalator hall with pedestrian access ramps, 2013

THE STATION NOW ARRIVING ...

2006   Like so many before it, this project was shelved. The reasons
are many and complex: lack of funding, changes in government and railway company policy, planning and highway
considerations, and revised passenger traffic forecasts. But
in 2006 a version of the final scheme emerged, with four
new platforms and a large glass box in front of the Three
Guineas.

2007–   By 2007 a much more ambitious plan was agreed, and
2013   work started in 2011. Over Easter 2013 the most conspicu-
ous part of the works opened to the public. New entrances

*North entrance view of the new escalator hall and transfer
deck, 2013*

The new escalators and roof supports, 2013

on both the south and north sides open into tall halls with ticket machines and stairs, lifts and escalators up to a very wide bridge or 'transfer deck', leading to platforms old and new. Numbers 1–3 are unchanged; a new platform 4 next to Apex Plaza gives additional capacity for trains to Waterloo and Gatwick; 4a and 4b became 5 & 6; the old 4 is 7 and the old 5 is 8. The old 6 & 7 have been abolished; 8 is now 9, 9 is 10, and 10 is 11, no longer a cul-de-sac but a through platform, as are the entirely new 12–15. The net increase over the 1900 layout is in fact only one platform (the GW had 10, the Southern station 4), but the new ones are more flexible. All platform lines will be electrified with AC overhead, except for 4–6 – which previously were the only electrified ones, on third-rail DC. The Vastern Road and Caversham Road bridges had to be widened (the latter in spectacular fashion when a whole massive deck was wheeled into place). One of the Cow Lane bridges has been enlarged, to

New southern entrance, 2013

be followed by the one carrying the main line. The old skew underpass to the east has reopened, as has the pedestrian subway, now a public path. A new signalling centre at Didcot serves the whole line from Paddington to Swindon and the Thames Valley branches. The Brunel Arcade, ticket office and Three Guineas pub remain, but the 1989 footbridge has been demolished. Away from the station, a new train depot has been built which will be able to deal with electric trains when they arrive.

The final part of the present scheme, just as important as increasing the station's capacity, will be the provision of new flyovers around the Cow Lane triangle. These will enable CrossCountry trains to proceed from Basingstoke to the northern platforms without crossing the main lines on the level; and freight from Southampton heading towards Oxford will similarly reach the slow (relief) lines.

GARE T.G.V.

Kenavon Drive, 2013

THE FUTURE

Reading station has been a massive job, but there is more to come. The lines from Paddington to Bristol, Swansea, Oxford and Newbury are to be electrified. So is Reading–Southampton and Oxford to Coventry, Bletchley and Bedford. Between Southampton and Birmingham, overbridges are being raised to accommodate larger freight containers. Crossrail may arrive. HS2 might have a stop at Old Oak Common near Acton, which would give potential fast connections to the North. If there is ever an HS3 it might come west and could conceivably connect with HS1 and mainland Europe. In anticipation of that day, someone has attached a sign to a lamp-post on Kenavon Drive pointing to 'Gare T.G.V.' (French for 'High Speed Train station') – evidently some enthusiast's holiday souvenir.

SOURCES AND FURTHER READING

My main source is *The Reading Mercury*, which can be viewed on micro-film at Reading Local Studies Library or online, digitised and searchable at the British Newspaper Archive. I have also consulted the *Berkshire Chronicle*, other newspapers and magazines, many books about the Great Western and other lines, biographies of Brunel, general local history, and travellers' tales. Old timetables and maps have been useful, as have the archives at STEAM – Museum of the Great Western Railway in Swindon and at the Brunel Institute at Bristol.

INDEX

This index includes people, places and topics that I think local and other readers might look for. I have not indexed words and names which occur frequently: Brunel, the Great Western and other principal railway companies, the railway mania, gauge wars, *The Reading Mercury* newspaper.

Two Rivers Press has been publishing in and about Reading since 1994. Founded by the artist Peter Hay (1951–2003), the press continues to delight readers, local and further afield, with its varied list of individually designed, thought-provoking books.